MY
THREE
DADS

My Three Dads

PATRIARCHY ON THE GREAT PLAINS

Jessa Crispin

THE UNIVERSITY OF CHICAGO PRESS

Chicago and London

The University of Chicago Press, Chicago 60637
The University of Chicago Press, Ltd., London
© 2022 by Jessa Crispin
Published 2022
Printed in the United States of America

31 30 29 28 27 26 25 24 23 22   1 2 3 4 5

ISBN-13: 978-0-226-82010-1 (paper)
ISBN-13: 978-0-226-60070-3 (e-book)
DOI: https://doi.org/10.7208/chicago/9780226600703.001.0001

Library of Congress Cataloging-in-Publication Data

Names: Crispin, Jessa, author.
Title: My three dads : patriarchy on the Great Plains / Jessa Crispin.
Description: Chicago : University of Chicago Press, 2022. | Includes
    bibliographical references.
Identifiers: LCCN 2021062384 | ISBN 9780226820101 (paperback) |
    ISBN 9780226600703 (ebook)
Subjects: LCSH: Patriarchy—Middle West—History. | Women—
    Middle West—Social conditions. | Middle West—Social
    conditions.
Classification: LCC HN79.A14 C75 2022 | DDC 306.0977—dc23/
    eng/20220118
LC record available at https://lccn.loc.gov/2021062384

♾ This paper meets the requirements of ANSI/NISO Z39.48-1992
(Permanence of Paper).

For my three husbands:
Nico, Christopher, and Noor

What is one to do with a Nazi father? Apparently the only solution is to reject him. If you speak of the need to integrate your identification with that father, you are immediately treated as a Nazi yourself. . . . In order to become a human being in the full sense of the term, we have to be able to discover, confront and own, the *Hitler in uns*, otherwise the repressed will return and the disavowed will come back in various guises.

JANINE CHASSEGUET-SMIRGEL

Memory operates as an unending sore.

STEPHEN FROSH

It is both reasonable and realistic to act as if another world were possible.

KATHI WEEKS

[0]

I am my father's son

HE APPEARED FIRST AS A PUDDLE. Liquid pushing up through the floorboards, rather than dripping down from above. I did not think much about it, just mopped it up with a towel and forgot about it until the puddle showed up in a new place.

How could I say this was strange, the whole house was strange. The first living, human occupant of a house that had remained vacant and boarded up for fifteen years, I struggled to adjust to it and it struggled to adjust to me. The animals of the neighborhood still considered it theirs. They found their way into the house one way or another: squirrels, baby possums, mice, stray cats. They wandered in through grates, through holes in the floorboards, through the basement. I shooed them all out with a broom, through the back door, until the heat and the wet of the summer warped the cheaply installed wooden frame so much that the back door no longer opened or closed without a few shoves.

Both the house and I felt permeable. There had been talk of a Kansas City economic revival, of a coming housing boom, and property started to be snatched up and rehabilitated, but the promised residents did not come. All over America, the whites of the white flight were leaving suburbs to reoccupy cities, but the whites of the Kansas City suburbs stayed put. Houses in the city remained empty, lots remained vacant and weedy. On every block in my neighborhood, at least three houses stood with plywood nailed across their windows and doors. There were large gaps between the houses, with the lots standing empty and overtaken by dramatic weeds. Whoever had bought this house lived in another state. They soon realized the investment was not going to pay off and halted the restoration process halfway through. There were new doors in old frames that still bore the marks of forced entry. The windows on the east side bore manufacturer stickers boasting of their energy efficiency, while those on the west side were so brittle and old that simply trying to open them would sometimes cause them to shatter.

This house, a rental, was the manifestation of giving up hope. I refused to get the message. I had returned not to the state of my birth but to within spitting distance of it. I could tiptoe right up to the border and retreat back to the safety of my house, but the house offered no real safety. Not even from the elements. Rain, wind, snow, cold, humidity—they all snuck in with the insects and the wildlife, sure this was their house too. I was spending a lot of time putting up weather stripping, hanging plastic across drafty windows, trying to claim a space that did not want me. I was insisting I belonged there, despite all evidence to the contrary.

So it did not help my sense of calm or belonging when the previous owner, long deceased, returned as a puddle, as knocking and whispering sounds in the kitchen, as wine glasses and towels and shoes moving around on their own, as a feeling emanating from the stairs to the second floor, as a basement door that would swing open whenever it cared to.

I shouted into my empty house, "If you're here, you're here, and I will try to deal with that, but if you ever show yourself to me, I will burn this fucking house down."

The dead seemed the majority demographic in the neighborhood. When I would explain to a Kansas City native where I lived, the response was usually, "Oh, the serial killer neighborhood." And a late-night internet search would confirm that, yes, just a few blocks over, past where I walked to get to the only grocery store, a mile and a half away, a man abducted young, gay men, he poured drain cleaner into their eyes and throats, he shocked their bodies with electricity, he drugged and suffocated them.

"You haven't heard of him," people told me, "because Dahmer happened around the same time, and Dahmer was prettier." There is only room in the American imagination for one sadistic predator of young men at a time. The predators of young women, on the other hand . . .

The house where the man killed so many men was razed, and I wonder if that unleashed their ghosts onto the neighborhood. To die in such agony, surely the energy of that rips outward for eternity. The former standard middle-class dream of a home, so normal looking, so white, in a respectable neighborhood, remains a gap between two other normal houses. If they too contain atrocities, they keep their secrets.

I tried to coexist with my one particular ghost, who was sticking around despite probably not having met a violent end. I admitted to myself that he and I had got off on the wrong foot, and that was my fault. On my first night after the move, alone in the hundred-year-old house with nothing more than one air mattress and one bottle of Jameson's whiskey, I had turned to Tinder for company. After twenty minutes of texting with a guy, I invited him over in the hopes he would either fuck me or murder me, and I wasn't sure which I preferred. This was before I had understood that the second floor was the previous owner's favorite spot, and here I was on the carpet, on all fours, getting fucked by a stranger more than ten years younger than me, right at the ghost's feet. Realizing my mistake after the ghost started to make his presence known, I tried to make amends by leaving the second floor almost entirely empty, giving him the space to pace endlessly back and forth as he seemed to like to do. I set up an altar in the living room, leaving out fruit and whiskey and lighting candles. I burned a lot of sage. I did not burn the house down.

But he would not meet me halfway. Soon muddy bootprints started showing up, coming in and out of the open basement door. The first time it happened I called the property manager and waited for his arrival on the porch. When he came in to inspect, he pointed out something I had overlooked in my panicked assumption that this time a living person had made their way into the house: a puddle of water on the top step of the basement stairs.

"Did you spill something?" I had not. "This doesn't make any sense." Well, I wasn't going to be the one to tell him.

While he inspected the rest of the house to make sure there was no intruder waiting in a closet to stab me, I stood out on the porch googling "Kansas City + ghost hunters" on my phone. Surprisingly, there were a lot of results.

A few days later, a team of ghost hunters was sitting in my living room. It was late. I had, for some reason, tried to make my house look less haunted from the outside, but it was hopeless. The porch was falling apart, the boards sagging and groaning under the weight of a body, and I had failed to pull up all of the fake plastic grass covering the rotting wood. There were remnants, too, of the plywood that used to cover the windows, though I had pried most of it off. With my crone nose and increasing age, now occupying a crumbling old house, I was in danger of becoming *that woman* in the neighborhood, the one you forbid your children from visiting when trick-or-treating on Halloween.

The team was one man and two women. The man was the spokesperson and the historian. If I chose to use their services, he would dig up the history of the house and find out who had previously lived here, if anyone had died, if the house was built on land where crimes against humanity had been committed. He made eye contact in a way that made me think "Scorpio rising" and be grateful for his female companions. One of the women had joined the team after employing the others for her own haunting. She had been friends with a man. He had wanted a romantic relationship, she had not, and she had had to reject him more than a few times. When he fell ill with cancer, she nursed him until his death. He refused to let her go, even in death, and moved into her house as a ghost. Almost every night she could smell his cigarette smoke and feel him touching her hair.

The other woman was a psychic. When I explained that I thought maybe I had a ghost, she said, "Oh yeah, he's right over there," and waved to the doorway to the second floor. It was the spot in the house I hated the most. There was no door hanging from the hinges, another casualty, I'm sure, of the abandoned rehabilitation. There was only a gaping darkness and a very narrow series of stairs leading up to an open loft space, and I was sure—I knew—that the ghost perched there, watching me. At night, I would turn off the lights from the far corner of the room, then have to walk past the doorway, quickly, to get to my bedroom. Every other light in the house could be blazing, but still I would feel an intense, dark pull as I passed those stairs. Most nights I kept my head down and held my breath. Never after dark did I even glance up to the landing at the top, afraid I would see the silhouette of my dead roommate standing there.

"So what is it that you all do?"

The man gave his sales pitch, despite there being nothing to sell. I learned there was a code of honor among ghost hunters, never to charge for their services. They were curious, is all. They were collecting information and proof of life after death. I would be helping them in their search, and if they could help me back by persuading my ghost to leave, that was a fair trade.

"Have you ever tried to contact your ghost? With a Ouija board maybe?"

"I'm not an idiot," I told him.

The psychic walked around the house and gave her assessment. Most of what she said confirmed my assumptions: the ghost was a middle-aged man who used to own the house and still felt very attached to the property. He thought of the second floor as his territory. He liked me, but he wished I would behave better.

That explained one of his first acts that got my attention: plucking a used condom out of the trash can and setting it down on the floor about a foot away. He wanted me to know he had been watching and that he disapproved.

"He watches you sleep. Also, the basement is filled with ghost children."

"Okay, maybe that's all I need to know for right now."

They got to the point. They wanted to spend a night in my house. They would set up cameras and see if anything I had reported moving around—glasses, towels, trash—could be caught on film. Or maybe he would show up himself, as a shadow or an orb or a full-body apparition. They would attempt to communicate with the ghost using EVP, they would track the ghost using EMF.

"Charlie, we call the ghost Charlie," I told them. Why Charlie? "We wanted something gender-neutral, so as not to offend."

If I wanted, they would then try to bless the house and encourage Charlie to move into the afterlife. But such attempts often failed, especially if the ghost still felt attached to something on this plane. Sometimes asking them to leave made them feel unwanted and grumpy, and the haunting activity would get more intense.

As I tried to decide, the EMF reader chirped and whistled. The readings were going up and down, up and down, even as we stood still. The psychic explained, "He is circling us now. He is wondering what we want." And then, they are gone, telling me to text when I decide what I want them to do, and I am left alone in the house, late at night, with Charlie. I head for the whiskey.

An email: "I thought you moved back to Kansas to deal with some ghosts anyway."

"I didn't mean for it to be literal."

A ghost is a story without an ending. Without resolution or closure, the story troubles and persists. Neither teller nor listener finds peace. You find yourself trying to carry the story forward, trying to push toward an ending so that you can be done with it. It seizes the imagination and worries it, overloading it.

But how does it, how *can* it, end? It's all unfinished business. The undiscovered will, the sentence cut short, the proclamation unproclaimed. The thing that wakes you in the middle of night with dread and the intense desire both to do and never to do, that thing keeps you awake nights even past your death. You can only wander around hopelessly. Now even if you had the nerve to say the thing you waited years, decades, to say, you no longer have the mouth or the tongue or the throat to form the words, let alone the right listener to hear them. All that is left is rattling pans, pushing open doors, creeping that woman out, in search of acknowledgment that you existed. It wasn't a great life or you wouldn't still be here, but it was a life that was lived.

And now your torment is tormenting others. People who didn't even know you. People who come through a hundred years later are rushing past darkened doorways or turning on a fan to avoid those inexplicable sounds, burning sage and leaving shards of black tourmaline around the house in an effort to make you not their problem anymore. And it's sad if you're still here because you got murdered or your daughter got murdered or you decided to murder and now your spirit finds no rest on this plane or any other, but it's something else if you were just so bad at being a person that you spend your death the same way you spent your life: useless, on the margins, making a pest of yourself. Who needs hell as the scene of eternal punishment when you have your own life?

I was getting a lot of dad energy from Charlie. This disapproval, this long list of unspoken rules, this very Midwestern version of masculinity that is all emotional constipation yet still strangely captivating, that leaves those around it scrutinizing every glimmer of the eye, every change in tone or inflection, looking for some sign of approval or affection or respect. The kind of masculinity that makes you think love is a thing to be earned through sacrifice and improved performance.

I was used to this type of man. Having grown up in rural Kansas, I had spent my whole life in his company. These have been the men in my family, my lovers, my friends. I had tried to please them or entertain them, tried to break through their hard exterior with love and jokes and food and stories. And in exchange for what? Certainly not love, certainly not approval. So that they would deign to stay in my presence, maybe. For the hint of a smile or the smallest gesture of affection.

But nothing I did pleased Charlie. If I left for a trip, upon my return the banging around in the kitchen would escalate. If I stayed home alone, I'd have the feeling of being watched. If a guest slept on the couch, they'd report hearing scratching sounds or waking up in the middle of the night with the feeling that their arms were being gripped by someone unseen. When I talked to him, I felt his presence nearer. If I ignored him, I'd hear him stomping around sullenly.

It wasn't just the real men in my life. It was all of the men who had come before. It was all of the men who had been used to teach me what love was, what god was, what pleasure was, what art was, what truth was. Despite getting so little back from them, I still spent my time in thrall of them, still trying to please some dead guy who wouldn't have liked me even when he was alive. Those men banged around my head the way Charlie banged around my house, and no amount of sage burning would get them out.

Built into the consciousness of every former farm kid is the idea of reinvention. I am not that, I am this other thing, I don't belong here. So you run away, you "get out," as they say, but the ghosts follow. Your body might move through space and time, but your inner workings are still entangled with where you come from. Spooky action at a distance. You find yourself recreating all your old traumas, you restage old scenes, you wander into a new setting reciting all the same old lines.

I felt a need to go back to see and deal with where I had come from. There were restless spirits I wanted to lay to rest. I had thought I could remake myself anew, but the gifts of my fathers were hard to shake. And I needed them to shake.

Sometimes I
scream so loud I
wake myself up

DAD ONE

THE FATHER

Joseph Pianalto

THE YEAR BEFORE MY FAMILY arrived in Lincoln, Kansas, another family was taken from it. A man wanted for murder, being chased by the police, took refuge in a farmhouse just off the highway. There was a family inside. In the ensuing standoff, with the sheriff parked outside and snipers on the surrounding buildings, the fugitive shot and killed the mother, the father, and their teenage son. And then he killed himself.

The newspaper articles list surviving family members. In a small town, family tends to stay close, so sisters, brothers, fathers, mothers, cousins, nieces, nephews, all get a mention. The grief still moves through the town. In the discussion of Truman Capote's *In Cold Blood* in my eighth-grade English class, the teacher remarked on the similarity of the murder in the book to the murder in real life. A girl, born only a few months after this part of her family was murdered, born into this grief, laid her head down on the desk as the teacher spoke.

My family were not the only new arrivals in this town where no one goes. Lincoln is one of those places you can live your entire life, but unless your family lived there your father's entire life and your grandfather's entire life you will always be a newcomer, always trapped in the process of arriving. It was and is a farming community, and you work the land your family has passed down to you. Unless you are farming or tangential to farming, there is little reason to show up here, few opportunities to find other forms of work. Only rarely will an opportunity open up and draw someone in from the outside. The need for a doctor, a new minister at the United Methodist Church, or, in my father's case, a county pharmacist.

Also rolling into this dot in the expanse, a coincidence of buildings in the flat farmlands in the center of the country, was the town's new art teacher with his wife and their two daughters. They arrived just a few years after us. My family came from Hays, a small university town in the west of Kansas, so my father could start a new job. The teacher and his family also came from Hays, although the two families were unknown to each other. My parents showed up with two little blonde girls in the back seat of their car. The art teacher and his wife brought two little blonde girls in the back seat of their car.

I think about the drive from Hays to Lincoln. I think about being the wife in the passenger seat, an entire life packed up in the station wagon behind me. It's only a ninety-minute drive, but time has no meaning on a Kansas interstate. It's a flat, straight line. When visibility is good, you can see everything the world has waiting for you laid out in the distance, and there is nothing there. Just the steady rhythm of the telephone poles, the occasional windmill to break up the landscape, maybe some cows in the fields.

Then the turn off the interstate and the quick drive down the highway to the new home. What would have been the sound in my mother's head? Only a few radio stations reach the town. There was a station that played endless soft rock, a country station, an oldies station, and the classical station down in the 80s frequency. My father usually preferred the classical station on these long stretches of western Kansas roads.

Approached from the south, the town starts with a church, white with gold accents. It was Lutheran, just on the outskirts, and mostly farmers went there. Then a tiny hiccup of a waterfall, where teens sometimes came to drink or make out, where hunters met before dispersing and slaughtering, where young girls not afraid of the snakes that hid in the grass climbed over rocks and waded into the water. Farther on was a plot where Christmas trees grew. This is where you will want to turn right to get to the old high school, since shut down and now vacant, but if you keep going straight you'll soon reach main street and the town's one traffic light, blinking red in all directions. There's a gas station to the right and a baseball field to the left. Go straight for a couple more blocks, and you'll reach the outer limits of the town, with its Pizza Hut and a burgers and milkshakes place, where if you ask they'll pump vanilla syrup into your soda, and the other gas station and a motel that usually houses only truckers.

If instead you turn right at the light, you'll see the town's business center. Pharmacy on the left, car dealership on the right. Two banks, across the street from one another. A small grocery store, run by the family with the nice house up in the north side of town. Off to the right, there's the post office where everyone calls you "hon" and the Carnegie library, a squat limestone refuge. There's a clothing store, a video rental place, a movie theater called without affection "The Roach," a cafe where the farmers who've come into town to see the bank about their debts gather for morning coffee. Then the park, the cemetery, which includes the grave of a man from out of town who died in the motel with no form of identification on him, and that is the entirety of the town. You can walk the circumference of the place in about an hour, looping around the high school, up north past the hospital, around to the old folks home, and then back.

Was there a profound "That's it?" in their chests? The same one that thrummed through me every time I obsessively walked the circle around the town, waiting for something to surprise me, for something to change? Or then, older, following the well-worn path of all the other teens cruising main street, U-turning through the park at the top of the street and again at the dead end at the railroad tracks at the bottom? All of us wearing a groove through the town, every detail committed to memory. This was the limit of my world. It wasn't like outside this little spot was wild prairie, stimulating the imagination. Fields abut the town. Outside there is only more production, more utility, more controlling and working the natural world to turn it into cash.

Not that the place lacks charm. With its tidy storefronts, its nineteenth-century limestone buildings, and its wide streets, one could picture Jimmy Stewart sauntering down the sidewalk in some never-made Frank Capra flick, using an unopened umbrella as a walking stick, a small-town lawyer determined to protect the interests of the good-hearted small-town folk against the greedy corporations focused solely on making a quick buck. He'd likely tip his hat to you.

Neither my mother nor the teacher's wife had any plans for work; they were here for their husbands. While their husbands built careers, they would make homes. For my family, in a small yellow house near the railroad tracks. For this other family, in a small white house not too far from the hospital.

Maybe the fantasy of small-town life hushed their fears. Maybe Jimmy Stewart wasn't like Santa Claus, maybe he did exist. And maybe the storied friendliness would be extended their way, like a cup of sugar from the neighbor or a mostly mayonnaise salad at the church potluck. Maybe there would be compensation for what has lost.

I asked my mother a couple years ago if it had been hard to leave Hays for a small, unknown town. While Hays was not a big city by any means, the difference between a town of twenty thousand and a town of twelve hundred is greater than the number of people. Hays had restaurants, movie theaters, professors, bookstores. It had a Woolworth's and a McDonald's. "Are you kidding?" she said. "I moved to a new place with two small children. In Hays, I had friends, I had a job." Left unsaid was what I remember from growing up in that house: in Lincoln, her life was her husband's. She was relegated to housework and some bookkeeping at his pharmacy. When my father sat down at the table, I asked him, "Was it hard for mom to leave Hays?" Without looking over to his wife or asking her directly, he answered, "No, she was fine."

I'll never forget the war waged on my mother's mouth when she heard his answer. It seemed she was hiding a sneer, biting back a retort, swallowing a scream, all at once behind a tense smile. My mother, usually so quick with the mean-spirited jab, the exasperated sigh, the joke that is definitely not a joke, still had trouble saying what she felt and what she meant when the subject was herself.

This second family came into my life when I was five. Mr. Pianalto taught art to the children from first grade through middle school. I don't remember when I started to grow attached to him in a different way than I did to my other teachers. I do remember his auburn hair. I remember his laugh. I remember he was funny, and often kind, but sometimes not. I remember his daughters, who had their mother's blonde hair.

The older daughter, Anne, was a little younger than me, the younger, Jennifer, a class or two below my little sister. I remember a photograph of Jennifer being tickled by her father, her mouth open as wide as it would go, wild with laughter. But I don't know if this photograph ever existed, if it was a freeze-frame of a memory, or if I created it in my head.

My entire world back then existed between school and home, and school became a refuge from home. School was easy. If you did what you were told, you were rewarded. There were rules, things were predictable, in contrast with how things were at home. I could never find my way at home, I could never find a way of being that would let me slide by unnoticed. I was casting about, looking for a surrogate family to substitute for my real one, the one I did not understand and could not live in, and Mr. Pianalto was there.

I remember him as a prankster. I remember him as laughing. I remember the anticipation of every Halloween. My sisters and I—by then there were three of us—were let loose on the town for hours in the dark, making our way to every house with a lit porch light, until the pounds of candy we collected in our bags (and the inevitable toothbrush from the dentist who lived around the corner) started to weigh us down. There was always excitement as we approached that other house, waiting to see what elaborate costumes and decorations Mr. Pianalto had set up this year. One year the scarecrow with the bowl of candy on his lap turned out not to be made of hay but to be Mr. Pianalto himself. As we tentatively reached our hands into the bowl, he snatched at them, a soft inanimate mass come to life, and we screamed and we giggled and we thrilled.

It's hard to say how or when the relationship developed. "Relationship" sounds like this story is going in a very specific direction, of grooming and violation, but it wasn't that. I was a high-maintenance child, and he helped with maintenance. I had trouble managing, even by age seven, even by age four, my anxiety and dread about the world. Home was not a refuge, just another place to need to escape. Mr. Pianalto noticed and he took care. That sounds like this story is going in a very specific direction, of the special teacher who dotes on the special student and helps that student blossom and achieve, but it is not that story either.

By the time I was ten, I was writing short plays. He would read them, and he once drew up a poster I could use if I ever put on a performance. I wish I could not remember the plays, but unfortunately I do. They were typical melodramatic ten-year-old-girl stories—a beautiful, special girl in a terrible family; she dies and then everyone is so very sorry for the way they treated her. She absolves them from heaven or, in one version, refuses to and god supports her decision. There was often a scene where someone smashed a plate. I loved the idea of the sound of a plate being smashed. I would never let myself smash a plate in real life, no matter how badly I wanted to hear the noise of that.

I remember one particular Monday. I was in the sixth grade. Monday was the day we had art class. Knowing I would see Mr. Pianalto, I wanted to look nice. I had a dress with spring green ruffles on the skirt, and one spring green ruffle along the neck. He had not seen this dress before. I put it on and wondered if he would like it. I was eleven.

I remember how weird it was that class had not started yet. The bell had rung a while ago, and yet Mr. Wallace had not moved from behind his desk. I had Mr. Wallace for homeroom, and he was very strict. We were all a little afraid of him. When he read us *Animal Farm*, he had done all the different voices, and that was funny, but somehow it was also scary. His face turned a purplish red when he was angry, and his voice carried. He was not one to be late starting class. I remember being uneasy about this, an unease not shared by my classmates, who kept talking and passing notes and snapping gum in the unexpected absence of authority.

Then our principal was in our room and he was speaking. I think there was a police officer with him. Or maybe it was a priest. It was a man in a uniform. I remember all of these things, and yet what I remember most are the blank spots. I remember being at my desk, and then I remember being in the back of the room pulling tissues out of the box, and I remember noticing the gap in time and being confused. Had I raised my hand for permission to get a tissue? It would have been very unlike me not to do so, yet I had no memory of asking for permission. One time in the first grade I had peed my pants because the teacher was not in the room. She was giving a stern lecture to another child in the hall for acting out, and I wouldn't let myself leave the classroom without first acquiring permission. It wasn't allowed. I sat there, arm raised, frantically waving, trying to get the attention of someone who wasn't even there. Standing up and walking to the back of the room without permission, even years later, was not something I would do. There was another blank spot, and then I was back at my desk, and tears were running down my face, and I was surprised at this. Why was I crying? Too many blank spots to remember.

The principal was still talking. I remember these sighs in between his words. Not sighs of boredom but sighs of someone looking for air. I remember him tilting his head back as he sighed, opening up his mouth like a fish sucking at food on the surface of the water. My brain stitched itself back together and I made sense of the announcement, of my reaction, of the faces of my classmates and friends around me.

Mr. Pianalto had not shown up at school, and neither had his two daughters. Someone was sent to the house, where bodies were then discovered. Everyone in the house was dead. Mr. Pianalto had taken his hunting rifle, he had shot and killed his wife and his two daughters in their beds. Then he sat down on the floor and he shot himself in the head.

I am sitting in the office of an important agent, and I'm thinking I wore the wrong lipstick. I forgot to bring the lipstick I was wearing with me from the terrible Brooklyn room I rented via the morally questionable AirBnB. It's a forty-five-minute train ride from the Midtown Manhattan office, too far to return to just for the sake of my fading glamour, so I go into the Sephora a couple blocks from the agency and panic-buy three lipsticks, only to notice as soon as I leave the store that they are all impossibly wrong. The one I put on is too wet and glossy, I have no idea if it is spilling out past my lipline, if it is maybe now down on my chin, and this guy represents important people who probably all know how to properly apply cosmetics and don't walk around with magenta smears across their chin.

I am trying to sell a story. I am trying to sell the story of the Pianaltos as a book. Why am I doing this. We're in a true-crime boom. We love to tell stories about dead white women. So I'm pitching this book, because if you're a writer, at least when something terrible happens to you or near you or to someone you kind of know, you can often transform that terrible act into a six-figure book deal with a possible Netflix option.

Every dead white woman is a story these days. An eight-part podcast or an eight-part Netflix docuseries or just a book. The hottest story of the year, the year before I sat here with lipstick bleeding into the cracks around my lips, was the story of a young woman murdered by her boyfriend . . . or was she? It inspired this other podcast I've been listening to, a young woman who killed herself in a strange way . . . or did she?

So I'm pitching the story of these dead women, and he keeps repeating it back to me, but with buzzwords swapped in. I say, "the claustrophobia of a rural community," and he says, "small-town secrets." I say, "people say he seemed depressed," and he says, "a tormented mind." But still, it's not quite working.

The problem with the idea I'm pitching is that there's no dot dot dot. It's pretty clear who killed who, and it's pretty clear why. There's nothing to chase or tantalize. The agent keeps looking around. I'm trying to hold his attention.

"Then there was this other murder."

He nods and adjusts some paper on his desk. "Go on."

"This year, the trial is coming up. See, there was this kid, he lived down the street from me, he ended up murdering his best friend."

He's back. "Was it drugs?"

"Well, there hasn't been a trial yet, but it seems they were involved in a series of small robberies and break-ins together. The actual death might have been an accident, he's not talking yet."

"I see, okay. How do we connect these."

"Well, he was the sheriff's son. And uh, the sheriff before him, he was the sheriff when the other murder happened, and people always said that he destroyed things at the crime scene."

"Wait, which crime scene."

"The Pianalto murder. The murder-suicide. He was the first one to respond. The rumors were he was burning something when the other cops showed up. They were friends. Maybe he burned a suicide note, no one knows."

"I'm getting it. You'll go back for the trial, you'll uncover this small-town mystery that makes you think of this other mystery, men and their secrets, the corruption of the police . . ."

"But I don't really want to go ba—"

"There's a Maggie Nelson book, you should model it on that. It could be the next *In Cold Blood*."

"But I hate *In Cold Blood* . . ."

He sits up, the meeting is clearly over. "Email me when you have a proposal."

It's not like I don't have plenty of other models for how to write this. Everyone who has the slightest connection to a murder is now writing a book about it. No longer relegated to the back of the bookstore in trashy mass market paperbacks printed on cheap yellowish paper, they are all released in hardback by prestigious presses. They fill the New Releases table at McNally Jackson bookstore. There's the one where the author's cousin is accused of murdering two girls, and she tries to prove him innocent. There's the other one where the girl she kind of knew in high school is murdered. There's the Maggie Nelson story of the dead aunt. There are pen pals and long-lost friends, nieces and step-cousins, all murdered or murdering, and the authors are eager to tell the tale. But, you know, in an elevated kind of way. Bloody, but make it *art*.

All of these writers must have felt like they got a lucky break when someone they kind of knew was stabbed to death or strangled and raped or shot in the back of the head. Finally, something to write about.

And why not tell the story? Doesn't telling stories make things better? By raising awareness or whatever. But we've been telling these stories of dead women for decades, centuries, and the bodies keep piling up.

I notice that the closer one is to the murdered, the less elevated the book. If it was your mother, your sister, your daughter, your lover, those books get tawdry covers and tawdry publishers. It's hard to elevate your prose when it comes out in a series of shrieks and sobs. And who wants to turn the once living, once breathing, once complicated and squishy, once beautiful and exasperating human being into just a story? Not just a story, but an entertainment.

What is my motivation for telling this story? Besides the fact that many days it is the only one banging around in my head? I sit down, try to write the proposal, but writing the proposal means tidying up something supremely messy. Turning blood into words, like some sort of demented, artistic Jesus. Less Jesus, more storefront magician. I keep thinking, people are going to be entertained reading this. They will only kind of pay attention to it on an airplane. They will speculate as to motivations on social media. They will distill this trauma into a hundred-word review on Goodreads. "So there was this teacher who one day took out his hunting rifle and . . ."

Then, just maybe, if I insert myself into the narrative in just the right way, if the book ascends to the god-level of Film and Television Adaptation, I can get Claire Danes to play me. She ugly-cries the way I do, she conveys the serious intelligence of a writer.

Writing is an act of tidying. It creates bone-hard structure out of floppy masses. It invents meaning where there is none, it domesticates the feral, it removes potency from the powerful. And isn't that the relief of it? I wanted to write the story of this murder so I could have a story to tell myself. One that was understandable and relatable. I wanted the story on the page so it would get the hell out of my head.

But I distrust a good story. I want to interfere, I don't want tidy, I don't want my reader to feel resolved and relieved at the end. I want everyone to see the mess.

Which is why I hate *In Cold Blood*. It's too good of a story. Back in the eighth-grade classroom, the book was exciting. When you come from Kansas, you rarely pick up a book about Kansas. You don't see your small-town life reflected back to you, unless it's turned sentimental (see: *Our Town*) or maudlin (see: *Our Town*). Rarely is our home made the setting of action, especially something exciting, like a murder and run from the law. Two men, two outsiders, invade a house in an innocent Kansas town and slaughter an entire family. Having heard that the farming family has a safe loaded with cash, they mean to rob them. Finding nothing, they murder them instead. The outsiders then go on the run, until they are hunted down by the law, found guilty by a jury of their peers, and executed for their crimes.

The story is almost mythical, and myths have a special hold on the mind. It is sweeping in its themes: lost innocence, big-city evil penetrating the quiet, simple goodness of small-town life, a society growing colder and more depraved. It inspired decades of retellings and supplements. Surviving family members, friends of the family, family and friends of the murderers, other writers from Kansas, writers who had nothing to do with Kansas, wrote memoirs, novelizations, comic books, documentaries, films, television shows, all trying to add a new perspective to—or cash in on—Capote's story of murder in a small town.

It couldn't have been more effectively cast. The wholesome-looking family, well groomed with bright, friendly smiles. They could all have been stars in a 1950s sitcom where the biggest problem the family faced was the boy breaking a neighbor's window with a ball as he practiced for the big game. The daughter's most pressing dilemma would be whose invitation to accept to the school dance. The parents would give wise counsel and exude a quiet, nondemonstrative kind of love.

Then we have the perpetrators, the criminal element. One, Perry Smith, is darkly complected, being half-Native. The other, Dick Hickock, looks much like the teenage boy he murdered, with his fair hair and strong chin, if only half of his face wasn't slightly caved in and twisted from a car accident and catastrophic head injury. Both Smith and Hickock bear scars from accidents of body and fate. Car crashes, a violent father, abandonment, poverty, military service, institutional abuse. You can tell just by looking at them that something is off. You're tipped off by a limp, say, or racial mixing, or eyes that don't quite line up. When Kansans saw the men's pictures in the newspaper announcing their arrest they must have thought, "Ah, of course, yes, the deformities of the body are manifestations of the deformities of the soul." That's big with Protestants.

"No one ever locked their front doors," one of the town's citizens said in one of the documentary miniseries that promised to tell the "real story" of the murders, but ended up telling the exact same story that always gets told. "That changed overnight."

There is a subset of Kansans that hate *In Cold Blood* and the industry built around this slaughter of a family. According to them, Capote was enchanted by the evil when he should have been focused on the goodness of the small-town community. He followed the more exciting story of murderers who take to the road, rather than the narrative dead end of the happy family. The victims, the town, we as Kansans, felt unseen by his book. It was our story, it happened to us, we should be the stars. (I think the protests were less about getting the story wrong and more about who got to tell it. An outsider. A queer, at that. A big-city type—just another violation by the evil that dwells outside the tidy home.) There is no greater betrayal than to speak a family's or a town's secrets in a small town like this. Whispered gossip within the community, okay. Broadcasting its faults to the outside world, unforgivable.

As much as we protest, though, the story of the murder of the Clutter family is convenient for us Kansans to tell. That's why we keep telling it. Not because it hasn't been told already, not because its original teller left anything important out. We tell it because it presents a story of Kansas and of family and of the small town as we want it to be told: the evil comes from the outside.

As a graduate of The Pianalto Family Management Program, when I heard about the Mom's March, taking place just a two-hour bus ride away, I knew I had to go.

The first Women's March had irked a certain segment of the population. Not only the big Washington, DC, march held to protest the inauguration of Donald Trump. Women congregated in smaller towns all across the Midwest, including several spots in Kansas. The same city squares in Wichita that had in the early 1990s hosted hundreds of anti-abortion protesters, waving hateful signs and swinging bloody baby dolls, an image forever seared into my brain via local television news coverage, now held space for a stronger congregation of women, singing songs and chanting, condemning no one to hellfire.

Someone had the idea to create a protest of the protest and bring together not the women of America but the moms. They picked Nebraska as the setting, not only for its symbolic power—you know, the "heartland"—but for its centrality in one specific female demographic: the stay-at-home, homeschooling mother.

Largely Protestant, largely Evangelical, the homeschooling family was an extreme version of the wholesome, churchgoing folk I grew up around. Generally more suburban than rural, more professional than agricultural, the homeschooling family incorporated new trends in the Evangelical lifestyle, from lifestyle missionaries to the Quiverfull movement. Some of those groups happened to find representation within my own extended family. They were the ones who, when I was a teenager asking for a Tori Amos album for Christmas, would give me a book about Jesus instead.

The Evangelical rhetoric was familiar to me, simply a stricter version of the Protestant way of life in which I had been raised. "I know your father" was a common form of introduction in my town. It was how we understood everyone's place. It was inevitable for me—I wore his face on my face, with the same crooked nose, same outsize ears, same light eyes. There was no escaping the association or the sense of possession.

The Sunday school education I received in the redbrick Methodist church just a short walk from my childhood home was as much an education about the family as it was about god. We would study cartoonish diagrams, with Christ holding an umbrella over the father—you can tell it's the father because he wears a suit and a fedora—who holds an umbrella over the wife, who has miraculously kept her tiny little waist despite multiple pregnancies (must have been the Richard Simmons workout videos that were popular at the time) and who in turn holds an umbrella over the children. What the rain represents is not stated, but we can guess. Chaos. Immorality. Sex. Drugs. The message was clear: If you find yourself outside of the family, through either exile or abandonment, there's nothing but rain waiting for you. Not even Christ will take your calls.

And there are a hundred ways you can find yourself outside of the family. If you can't behave, if you can't perform heterosexuality (or now that even churches in small towns have rainbow flags in their windows, if you can't perform heteronormativity), if you find yourself the subject of unwanted attention by a father or a brother or an uncle, if your parents find themselves lost in drink or pills, if you get hit one too many times, you'll find yourself outside this zone of protection. And I couldn't behave, and my mother couldn't redirect her resentment about finding herself in a new town with a six-month-old baby and no support system back on her husband, because consciously hating your husband in this kind of structure is an existential threat. So I found myself with a little unwanted attention, but never enough to push me fully outside of the family. I was outside the zone of protection, but I couldn't get free of the overlying structure. Here's me—half rained-on, water filling up my shoes, but my hair is still looking great—trying to get either fully in or fully out.

The Evangelical homeschooling family had a similar structure, except that nothing, not a single goddamn thing, existed outside the hierarchy of the family. There was no school, because even the theory of evolution was part of that sinful rain. There was no secular entertainment, no journalism or media, no friends or strangers. The homeschooling father didn't hold an umbrella over his children. He sealed them into a waterproof pod.

So yeah, I took the bus up to Omaha to go spy on these nice church folk, all these gold star families and Christrock family bands. There was a full day of activities planned. They had booked an entire arena. Sarah Palin was the keynote speaker. I wanted to get there early to get a good seat.

I arrived and saw an empty parking lot. I walked into the arena, and my footsteps echoed. Surely I had come on the wrong day. Where the hell are all the moms?

There were a few. There were a handful of booths set up in the hallways, some instructing me to pray the rosary to end abortion, others selling stacks of self-published Christian novels about good families in a bad world. I was handed a rubber fetus, lifelike in a way that made me worried about everyone involved in its production, and I was lectured to about the threats the modern Christian family must face.

I settled into a folding chair to listen to the speakers address a mostly empty room with an enthusiasm that suggested they were all hallucinating rapturous crowds. They sermonized about the corrupt secular culture that degraded women and children. Here, though, the enemy was not the pussy-grabbing president but his rival/close friend Hillary Clinton. Not because she had won the popular vote in the 2016 election, nor because her husband had been accused, more than once, of sexual assault. It wasn't even her warmongering as secretary of state or her association with men like Harvey Weinstein and Jeffrey Epstein. Her book about society's obligation when it comes to raising the next generation, *It Takes a Village*, published twenty years before, was still making some people absolutely furious.

"It doesn't take a village," more than one speaker that day said. "It takes a family." A woman was manning a booth with dozens of copies of her book *Who Needs a Village? It's a Mom Thing* stacked around her. As I walked around the convention center trying to find a cocktail or at least some piss-tasting light beer to get me through this experience, I met many such moms. (No booze, though. The wine-mom economy had not yet infiltrated the homeschool-mom demographic.) The word "mom" in the event's title was strategic, conjuring up images of economy-size bags of Ruffle's potato chips from Costco, six- to eight-capacity vehicles, and mall fashion. She's a woman who will love you until it makes you uncomfortable, who will give up her free time and life and health and money for you, and then will never let you forget that sacrifice.

As I was waiting for Sarah Palin's keynote address, a woman sat down a few chairs to my right. She looked remarkably like my aunt Barb, with capri pants and the sensible haircut of a mother without much time in a bathroom by herself. She told me she had driven over from Iowa, where she homeschools her boys, because she was tired of feminists telling her "how to be a woman." I didn't tell her I originally left Kansas because I was tired of everyone around me telling me the same thing. But we did find some middle ground in our frustration that feminism these days just seemed to be about how to get a better job. *Lean In* and all that. She told me she didn't want to work. "I don't either," I told her, but I think we meant it differently.

The women there reminded me of the women I had known all of my life. Like my aunt, who refused to let her children watch *Casper the Friendly Ghost* because it contradicted Christian teachings about the afterlife. Or my other aunt, who never seemed to have a personality when her husband was around, and he was always around. She has a silvery laugh, which I remember hearing three times in my lifetime. Or my friend's mother, who forced her daughter to return the shirt she had borrowed from me in high school, unworn, because red and shiny was immodest and showy, even with long sleeves and a high neckline. Women who baked with Crisco and had demented ideas about what constituted a "salad," women who wanted to tell you personal and revealing stories about other women you had never met, women who would give you their meaty left arm if you said you really needed it. Women I happen to like, tremendously.

But there was an edge to the voices, as they spoke about the world outside of their homes. It was a world they could no longer understand, a world gone mad. They love their families, and they will use their love and their megachurch and their homeschool coursework as a shield to protect their children from depravity, from the science of climate change, from gender dysphoria. And that clear division between public and private, mine and yours, goes both ways. Whatever happens out in the world, with its porn stars and its urban violence, is not their (or their children's) concern. They don't care what goes on behind your closed doors (unless it's sodomy, of course), and what happens behind theirs is absolutely none of your business. I heard those exact words on a podcast about a Minnesota lesbian couple who murdered their six children and themselves, spoken by a neighbor after one of the kids escaped in the middle of the night, banged desperately on his door, and begged not to be forced to return home. The neighbor was explaining why he sent the child back to her mothers and convinced his wife not to call the authorities. "It was none of my business."

So that's what bothered me about *In Cold Blood*. The idea of danger drifting into town in the form of a couple freewheeling strangers with nothing in their pockets and bad intentions in their hearts. We always, for the record, locked our front door. My family might describe our small town as the kind of place you could leave your front door unlocked—someone says it in every small-town true-crime story ever told in any medium— but we always locked our doors. And it's important to clarify what that means, because when you lock your doors at night, to keep bad things at bay and protect yourself and your family, you're not excluding the thing most likely to do you harm. You're locking yourself in with it.

The first time I saw the movie *The Shining*, I thought it was a pretty good ghost story. Like a lot of heterosexual women, I thought Stanley Kubrick was the greatest filmmaker ever, because I had been told that by many men I had been sleeping with, men who also told me they took film more seriously than I did.

"Do you see? The typewriter, it changes color. So brilliant."
"What does that mean?"
"No one knows for sure."
"Oh. Okay."
"Such a genius."

The second time I saw the film, I understood it to be a very straightforward, not in any way supernatural film about a man trying to murder his wife and child. I had trouble breathing when I watched it.

Somewhere between these two viewings, a span of eight years or so, I got a phrase stuck in my head. It would come to me when I was working, when I was falling asleep, when I was cooking, when I was just walking around. "Her bare feet." I could see, in my mind, someone saying these words, a man, in a brown uniform and hat, saying this into a microphone, but I couldn't quite place it. Maybe it was from a film, but I could not conjure any of the surrounding imagery. This went on for months. "Her bare feet," I would think to myself, picking up a box of clementines at the grocery store. "Her bare feet," I would think, waiting for a crosswalk signal to change.

One day I put on *Paradise Lost,* a documentary about the murder of young boys in a small town. Three teenage boys who listened to heavy metal were tried and convicted for the murders, despite there being no evidence tying them to the scene. A follow-up documentary would suggest the real killer was probably one of the boys' stepfathers.

I had seen the documentary before, years before, when it had first come out. I had been moved by it, but it had moved quickly through my head. Now, I decided for unknown reasons to rewatch it. I was living in Berlin at the time. I remember I was sitting in a chair by the living room window. Later the chair would reside by the bookshelves, after I bought a chaise lounge and had to rearrange the room to make it fit. In the documentary, we see footage of a concerned townsperson, about to be interviewed for the television news. She is excited to be talking to a reporter, she is asking when it will air. When the interview begins, her demeanor changes immediately, back to performing a role of grief for the outside world.

I think the footage was meant to be damning, showing her display of concern and mourning as in some way insincere. But I know how flattering and exciting it is to be paid attention to, even if the reason for that attention is exploitative and sensational, when you come from an oft-ignored small town.

It reminded me, suddenly, of a VHS tape we had in my childhood home. On the day they discovered the Pianalto family's bodies, school continued. To shut down an entire school system, a lot of phone calls had to be made, even in a small town like ours. A couple hundred parents had to be reached. As those calls were made, we were sent out for an endless, very grim recess, children left alone to try to piece together what had happened. There was crying, but there were also cries of exhilaration from the playground.

When we were finally let go, it wasn't just our parents waiting for us. There were also news vans, men with microphones, things we had only ever seen on television. It had been almost fourteen years since the family outside of town was wiped out, and none of us had been alive back then. I have no functional memory of being with my mother as she spoke to the journalist, but I remember the newscast. Me in my white and green dress, my pale, stricken face zoomed in on to illustrate the impact of the tragedy; I leaned heavily on my mother's body as she spoke of the shock of it all. We sat around that evening before the news, with the blank VHS tape in the VCR, ready to record this first and maybe only encounter with the larger world.

Watching the documentary, I finally remembered the source of the words in my head. The local sheriff had also spoken in that three-minute news clip, describing the scene at Mr. Pianalto's home. The wife had been in bed, he said, "her bare feet" indicating she was killed as she slept. The full force of the memory returned. It wasn't that I had repressed it, I had merely refused to remember. I had begun to refuse the moment it happened, and that refusal continued until a few seconds of a documentary about something else reminded me, and I was overtaken by the memory, which has since refused to leave. I wonder what it had done in the interim, worming around below my conscious mind.

When I saw *The Shining* again, as Wendy weakly swings the bat at her menacing, slowly advancing husband, hoping he will just stop, just stop being this and go back to being a husband and a father, I did not see a man possessed by the evil spirit of a hotel. I saw a man stalk and hunt and try to kill his family. Because that is a thing that happens. It happens so often there is a term for it, "family annihilation." Three women a day in America are killed by their romantic partners, fifty thousand women a year worldwide. It happens so often it is obvious and boring.

When it happens in your neighborhood, I mean. When it happens in your film, in your tabloid television, in your podcasts, it's fucking thrilling.

But that boredom is how we have a documentary like *Room 237*, where a bunch of men, and one woman, speculate on what *The Shining* is actually about. Kubrick was such a genius, it couldn't simply be a story of another family annihilator, something so pedestrian. It can't be about how murdering your family is so common it is practically tradition. "I *and the others* have come to believe your heart is not in this," one family annihilator in *The Shining* (who killed his wife and two daughters with an ax) tells the potential family annihilator Jack, played by Jack Nicholson. Even within the film, the murdering of wives is casually reported on the news, as an Aspen woman disappears on a hunting trip with her husband.

But no, each of the people in *Room 237* insists, the film is actually about the genocide of Native Americans, or actually about the Holocaust, or actually about demons wanting to have sex with humans, or actually Kubrick's confession of helping to fake the moon landing.

Trying to figure out what a work of art is *about*, like a thesis statement or a trick or a puzzle that needs solving, is a way of protecting yourself from it. But all of these theories, men speculating that Wendy is not a hunted wife but a representative of all the murdered European Jews or all the slaughtered Native tribes, seem like deflections from the knowledge that sometimes men kill their families.

But we try to protect ourselves from the information we need to survive all the time. I had wondered, now that there have been a couple decades of domestic abuse awareness campaigns, whether the Pianalto story was told any differently back home. The local amateur historian, who like all good people who occupy this place in a small town uses equal parts documentation and gossip to tell her stories, was trying to tell me about a tar-and-feathering that happened in 1911. A young woman teacher was run out of town for possibly sleeping with her students. They poured hot, thick tar over her body, and when it was peeled off her skin came off in sheets. I tried to redirect her back to the murder-suicide; she of all people would know what everyone thought. The same answers came back: "the drug world," gambling, murder, whatever. There was a vague idea that Mr. Pianalto had pissed off "the wrong people" with his drug-free campaign at the high school. It's the kind of violent fantasy that small-town folk have about big cities, a sludgy wash of evening-news paranoia, all of those films from the 1990s where someone gets off the interstate at the wrong moment and finds themselves trapped in an inner-city war zone, and half-remembered scenes from that one time they watched *Taxi Driver* twenty years ago.

But, she said, there was this one time. When Mr. Pianalto had come to pick up Mrs. Pianalto and the children, and there was fear in Shirley's face. You know, maybe there was something . . . but also probably it was a drug-related hit.

There is a chuckle in *The Shining*, when the hotel owner explains what happened with the last caretaker. "He"—chuckle—"killed his family with an ax."

My sister had just had a baby, so stories were coming out. As we sat around the kitchen table with the other women of the family, we heard stories for the first time, of us as children, of our mother, of our grandmothers, of people in our family we had never known. Like the one about my great-grandmother, who had recently left her husband, who was beating her, and was at the town dance with another man. Her son—my grandfather, twelve or thirteen at the time, they thought—was standing around outside when he saw his own father approach with a gun, asking where his wife was. My grandfather quickly made up some story, sent him off in the wrong direction, and then helped my great-grandmother escape to safety. Then.

"There was that time"—chuckle—"when Tom tried to kill you." This was said to my mother.

My sister and I sat silent, while the other women at the table laughed. My mother, a young child, barely yet able to form long-term memories, had been taken aside by her brother, who was a few years older. He fed her the contents of the medicine cabinet. My mother had to be taken to the emergency room.

"What happened to him?"

"Oh, nothing. He was a kid. Oh, right, and then he did it again a few months later, right? Then back to the emergency room!" More laughter, more stories, like the one about the time my uncle held an air rifle flush to my mother's back and pulled the trigger.

I remembered how as children my older sister and I would howl whenever our uncle came over. No one ever said anything about him, but we both seemed to sense something off, even when quite young. Even at the age of two or three, we were resolute, we would not be touched or held or left alone with him. We would shriek and cry. The people around us would laugh, they would bribe us with food to get us to sit still, to let him hold us. My mother would sometimes ask him to watch us for an evening, and we would try to disappear behind our books.

I don't remember my mother's face, if she tried to laugh along or if she found herself unable to do so. I do remember my sister's, turned half away from the other women of my family. She looked wary, with only half of her mouth curled into a smile.

In the weeks and months after Mr. Pianalto murdered his

family and killed himself, there were whispered alternative theories. Maybe he had been into drugs? And maybe they all had been killed by a drug dealer? Maybe he had had gambling debts? And maybe they had been killed by a bookie? Maybe it was a robbery? Myths retell themselves all the time—maybe *In Cold Blood* needed a volume two? People look for reasons, and no reasons could be found: no money trouble, no obvious signs of addiction, no treatment for mental illness. Everyone in this town worked hard to avoid the conclusion that sometimes men just murder their families.

For years I became obsessed with true-crime stories of men who kill their lovers, their wives, their children, their families. It became almost reassuring. This is how the world works. This is what happens. Mr. Pianalto wasn't such an anomaly after all. He is part of a tradition.

But I think I was also trying to find Mr. Pianalto in the statistics and in the psychological profiles. The person I knew could not have killed his family, so who was this other person? I went to the Wikipedia page "Notable Familicides" and read through the list of other men who killed their families. Is this who he is? Is he Chris Watts? Is he William Parente? Is he Jean-Claude Romand? In one act, he wiped out my memory of him, made it all suspect, because the person who is tender and warm and funny is not the person who puts a gun to a young girl's head, certainly not his daughter's. So maybe he's just one of these monsters. Except maybe William Parente was also tender and warm and funny. Maybe he too was careful with people who needed care. Maybe he thought of his daughter as precious, right up until he obstructed her airway.

I was doing much the same thing the people in my town were doing, trying not to admit I'd loved a murderer. And this town, where a girl in my class was sent regularly to school with bruises that everyone politely ignored, where another girl was being raped by her mother's boyfriend almost every night, also politely ignored, where suicide, drink, and beatings happened quietly behind front doors and pretty little gardens, should have known the way things inside a house can get all twisted up.

The dream of the
house in the house

Not the loss, but rather the extraordinary attraction of the
home is what threatens the subject.

ELIZABETH BRONFEN

I've polished this anger and now it is a knife

CATHY LINH CHE

I HAVE LOCKED myself in the gas station bathroom.

I have this fantasy of the intact family. I think the problem
must be me. It must be my sullen insolence that broke up the
picture-perfect Christmas card. That is who they are when
I am not there—I have seen the photos, with the bright smiles
and apple cheeks, everyone in red and green sitting in front of
the lit-up Christmas tree. But when I'm there—and I am rarely
there—I muck it up somehow. The photos from those holidays
are a little different. Smiles go off-kilter. Eyes reveal frustration.
It must be me who creates this dissonance. Still, I reenter my
family from time to time with absolute optimism that we will
get along. I can control myself, my responses, my behavior, and
I can be in there too, in the perfect photos, not the ones with
gritted teeth.

Which is how I ended up on a road trip from my haunted house in Kansas City to West Virginia with my parents as a forty-year-old woman. But less than twenty-four hours into the weeklong trip, my old ailment, my involuntary bulimia, starts up again, and I am trying to hide it. From childhood on, even before the death of the Pianaltos, I had this trouble keeping food down and in. It all came splashing out again. I was always making a mess and always desperate to hide the mess.

They say jokingly that around your parents you revert to the position of a child, no matter what stature or dignity you've attained in adulthood. We regress to our bratty teen selves, rolling our eyes and sighing dramatically and slamming doors. They in turn treat us like we're the children they remember, incompetent and helpless. As a child I was sick, messy, screaming. Here I am as a middle-aged woman, again sick, messy, screaming. Making a mess and desperate to hide the mess.

In the back seat of my parents' minivan, I recreate my teenage self, who was always hiding under headphones. Rather than Nine Inch Nails and screeching PJ Harvey bootlegs, though, this time I distract myself with podcasts, because I love a good zeitgeist. The most popular podcast the day I throw my suitcase into the back and settle in for four full days of driving and antiquing is *Dirty John*, about a con man who manipulates a woman into marrying him, tries to take all of her money, becomes obsessive and controlling, and after she leaves him begins to stalk her adult daughters. Everyone loves it. They're turning it into a TV show.

Violence is part of this woman Debra's family tradition, and the story branches out from one abusive relationship into a whole network. Before the con man, Debra had already lived through a series of failed, nasty relationships. She had already years ago lost her sister Cindi to domestic violence. When Cindi started to complain about her marriage—her husband was trying to control her, having wild fits of jealous rage—their mother told her it was normal, she was wrong to feel afraid. If a man can't stand to watch you leave the house without him or wear a bikini on the beach, it just means he's devoted to you. Cindi went back to her marriage only to have her husband put a gun to the back of her head and pull the trigger. Their mother testified in court for the defense, arguing that this man had been a good husband to her daughter, who was now dead with a hole in her head.

Down one daughter from the violent act of marriage, she then fails to protect her second daughter. Debra's stories of her own husband's complicated lies and her missing money and the way he tries to isolate her from her daughters must, her mother thinks, be exaggerated. Meanwhile the con man is buying chloroform, duct tape, zip ties.

The podcast has a catchy theme song that rattles through my head. But there's something else rattling through my head: an offhand remark made by Debra's youngest daughter, Terra. She and her sister had taken a dislike to their mother's new husband immediately, and when Terra sees this man playing with her nieces and nephews at Christmas, she becomes "hysterical." She uses the word, her mother uses the word, her grandmother uses the word, to describe the overwhelming physical reaction she has to seeing a man she on some level perceives as a threat in close proximity to vulnerable family members she loves. She sobs uncontrollably, she can't breathe, she screams and wails.

Later, she starts dreaming about him attacking her, about being forced to kill him to save her life. Later, he will attack her. Later, she will be forced to kill him to save her life. Being "sensitive," she somehow picks up on the ripples of this future event, and the unconscious knowledge overwhelms her body.

In my haphazard packing for this road trip, I grabbed a few books at random from the to-be-read pile that is more like a mound that is more like a mountain. One is a history of hysteria. I am hysteric in the back of my parents' van, reading about hysteria. This book from twenty years ago, when writing about hysteria was what all the feminists were doing, especially the French ones, came through time to explain my life right now to me. It's embarrassing! It's embarrassing to be a feminist in your forties still thinking deep thoughts about hysteria. This is second-wave shit, this is teenage shit. And yet, here we all still are, in our neat little houses puking our guts out or falling to the floor in fits, using the same societal structures as centuries ago and wondering why we're all so upset.

Hysteria used to mean a womb out of place. The uterus, dissatisfied, dislodges itself and wanders the body, causing havoc as it shoves aside the other organs and releases its vapors, which I visualize as something between the air shimmering over a highway on a hot day and the squiggles coming off a cartoon skunk. But really, it means a woman out of place. Hysterical girls in nineteenth-century France, often raped or beaten or molested by family members and forced to keep the abuse secret, kept their mouths shut, but their bodies betrayed them. They collapsed and convulsed and were sent away to Paris asylums. There they became stars, performing their fits for doctors, philosophers, artists. Before, no one paid attention to their suffering. Now, in front of medical staff and spectators, they could turn it into grand art. After a while, it can be difficult to distinguish between suffering and the performance of suffering.

The body of a hysteric is like a haunted house. The knockings and bangings articulate what can't be said: There is something wrong here. The calm surface cannot remain unruffled. What doesn't come out in words will come out in vomit, shit, tears, screams. Or unseen forces, pelting stones.

We always end up back here. Despite centuries of women arguing we should have other ways of structuring our families, our cities, our love lives, our houses, because the way we have is literally killing us, we always end up back at the family sealed off in a home. It is hard to fight the presumption that romantic love should be coupled with a mortgage, that the person you sexually desire should help you parent your children, that each domestic space should be a fully functioning productive unit. Any living arrangement that is not with a person with whom you have emotionally, financially, domestically, reproductively, sexually melded is merely a pause, a temporary setup that will inevitably yield to the person who fills all those roles. It doesn't help that our entire world, from the structure of our cities to our legal rights, reinforces the importance of the couple paradigm.

But then, what's worse, to be inside the couple with all of its obvious compromises and threats, all of its pains and boredoms, or to be outside of it? To be outside of the couple is to lack the basic rights, the intimate companionship, and the financial benefits that come with marriage. Marriage is an instant structure to lock yourself into, an easy series of decisions about what to do with your life and how to make it work. At the same time, you make yourself legible; the world around you understands your place and the role you play when you announce yourself as wife, as husband, as mother, as father.

The couple, Freud said, is the building block of civilization. It creates stability and a drive toward the future. To live outside the couple, then, is to find yourself one of the barbarians. So why not lay siege?

The deaths of the Pianaltos, in true Midwestern fashion, were never directly discussed again. We went to a memorial service, which at no point mentioned the method by which an entire family was eradicated overnight. We had one conversation with a minister, who I remember answering a child's question—could we ask Mr. Pianalto why he did it when we saw him in heaven?—with "Men who kill themselves go to hell, not heaven." We heard whispered gossip and overheard conversations at the beauty salon or the hardware store. And that was it. No trauma counselors, no family discussions. We as children were left to find ways to understand what had happened on our own.

Ultimately what I understood it was this: loving someone could get you killed. But there weren't a lot of places to go with that information at eleven years old. Desire is horrifying for everyone, especially those with late-developing breasts, but it was a long time till I found an entry point to start thinking through all the ways I associated love and comfort with death.

It was a miracle, then, that I found queer theory on the high plains. In the 1990s, our town had no bookstore, no MTV, no internet that wasn't a long-distance call on the dial-up. The only postwar literature in the local library was Stephen King, Clive Cussler, and Mary Higgins Clark. After the movie theater closed, having only played, to my memory, *King Ralph* and *Goonies* on endless repeat, the closest cinema was forty-five miles away. The closest bookstore that wasn't a Waldenbooks was a hundred and fifty miles. If something was not covered in the small regional newspaper or on the six o'clock news, it might as well not be happening.

I was desperate for signs of life, and I found them in the magazine rack at the HyperMart in Topeka, Kansas. We would stop there to refill giant gulps of Diet Coke, load up on discount housewares, and buy industrial-size packs of paper towels. I would tear the subscription cards out of every magazine I could find and ask my mother to write checks with the amount deducted from my allowance ledger. We girls were not allowed access to cash. Every purchase we made had to be ratified and transacted by my parents. Luckily they thought magazines were educational, and didn't pay too much attention to the covers, and soon music magazines, gay magazines, fashion magazines, cooking magazines, travel magazines, news magazines, men's magazines, feminist magazines all came pouring in.

These magazines would tell me what the rest of the world was like. It seemed better out there. At the very least, it seemed there was less Air Supply being played on the radio out there. But more importantly, having been raised within a Midwestern monoculture, I discovered there were other ways one could live a life. I was introduced to the writing of David Wojnarowicz, Larry Kramer, and Paul Monette. Queer culture spoke to me in a way feminism did not. This was the time of Riot Grrl third wave; there were philosophical arguments about whether one could wear lipstick and still be a feminist, debates between those who thought we could fuck men into feminist enlightenment and those who thought we should practice lesbianism for political reasons, go live off the land and never talk to men again, articles on environmentally conscious menstrual products. I had the feeling that love and desire would ultimately kill me, albeit via a bullet to the head rather than a virus—we were on different wavelengths just then.

In gay literature and queer theory, I read about what it was like to be ejected from the family, sent into exile because of who you fundamentally were, about how being marginalized from the family left you unprotected within society. Because there is no American society, there is only American family. Without a family, you are kind of on your own.

The stories of the AIDS crisis were not of young gay men tragically dying in the warm embrace of their families, no matter what "teach straight people about AIDS" movies like *Philadelphia* wanted you to believe. They were stories of people disowned by parents and siblings, being taken care of by lovers, exes, friends, strangers, a community of care that sprang up to compensate for what the family withheld.

The task of replacing what the family provides is enormous. It's not just the rights granted to those lucky enough to sustain a stable love life formalized as marriage—like who is allowed to make decisions for you when you are incapacitated, or who gets to stay in your apartment after you die, or who gets access to health insurance and immigration assistance, or who gets custody of your children. It's also who will touch you when your body smells like decay, who will put socks on your cold feet, who will fall asleep in the chair next to your hospital bed, who will vouch for you and make introductions to help you make your way in society, who will take responsibility for you, who will forgive you when you fuck up endlessly, who will take you in. In some places, queer communities were able to provide that for each other. Other people were not so lucky. Lost somewhere between family and community, with no society to help them out, they died alone, anonymous, without being checked on or cared for.

Outside of marriage, family, or romantic love, it is difficult to find the same sustaining warmth and legal infrastructure. No wonder, then, that people burrow their way into this refuge. So much easier, despite the increasing instability of romantic relationships, than building those bonds elsewhere. It's like musical chairs, everyone frantically trying to find someone's lap to land on. Few ask what happens to those who are kicked out in every round, those who are deemed unlovable or unfuckable.

"I like to think of myself as a spinster."

This was said to me by a married woman. A woman who has been with her husband her entire adult life. A woman who is financially supported by her husband so she can spend her days writing and making salads.

I moved to squeeze the lemon wedge over the plate of oysters between us, but she stopped me. "Not on my half, please. I like mine naked." I dumped lemon and vinegar and hot sauce all over my half.

"But you're married."

"Oh, I know! But I like to think of myself as independent. It's so glamorous. Well, like your life, how exciting everything must be. You can do whatever you want!"

A violent twitch went off within me. My old need to perform my suffering, my hysteria. I wanted to dispel the fantasy of what a life with few ties actually looks like. I wanted her to see the struggle, because freedom has a context. Hot, angry stories came out, of financial precarity, of holidays spent alone, of having to drag myself to the emergency room at 2 a.m. wrapped in a blanket because I was in too much pain to get into my coat, only to be cut open without anesthesia to drain an abscess and then to spend hours alone in pain and then to wait in the lobby high on fentanyl and exhaustion for fifteen minutes for the taxi that would take me to a home where only a cat and a ghost awaited my return, and where I'd soon receive a ten-thousand-dollar hospital bill because I couldn't afford health insurance as an unmarried writer. She awkwardly excused herself. I ordered another glass of champagne.

It was too much, and it's not even how I think about my life, as one of pure struggle. As much as I overemphasize the difficulty of living a life on my own, I also over-romanticize my independence, from Christmas afternoons spent at dive bars with all of the other lonely scumbags to booking travel to Budapest whenever I can scrounge up the money or miles for airfare. I romanticize because it's the only way sometimes to continue to convince myself that this is a life worth living, and I perform the hysteria because how dare someone shielded by the full protection of capital and family and property tell me how great my life is.

Everyone who has been kicked out of their family or has to move away from them or finds themselves at protracted odds with them talks about their "family of choice," but the family of choice is rarely as solidly connected as the family of birth. There are gaps. One can fall.

The family of choice means well, but as everyone moves around for jobs and school these days, there is no central place to gather. We tell ourselves online contact is the same as in-person contact even though it clearly isn't. Even the weirdos feel compelled to couple up eventually and vainly try to create a happy home despite having no idea what one even looks like outside of television. Sooner or later your "sister separated at birth" gets a baby or a puppy, and there you are, on the lowest rung of their priorities. All of a sudden the only time they're in touch is when they are liking your Instagram picture of the beautiful tacos you made for yourself and then ate alone in front of the television. Families of choice rarely create that marital level of emotional or material protection, nor does the United States government recognize your "we might as well be married" best friend as an actual spouse when it comes to establishing legal rights.

One of the purposes of hysteria is to sully the clean surface, to refuse to let things just be pretty and calm. And once you start that performance, it is difficult ever to stop. You will forever be the clown at the cocktail party, the scowl in the group photo, the low moan underlying the laughter.

I wonder if this is why I thieve from families. Invited into tastefully decorated homes, I have a bad habit of shoving things into my purse. Small things. A bar of soap from under the bathroom sink. A book of matches from the armoire. A block of cheese from the refrigerator. Four benzodiazepines from the medicine cabinet. A pot of nail polish from the make-up drawer. Pens from anywhere, as long as they are somewhat nicer than a Bic. "You have so much," I mutter darkly about my friends as I slap deli meat between two slices of bread and shove it into my pocket. "You probably won't even notice it's gone." I would never want to take something from a single woman, but I have a sense of entitled resentment toward the married. I want, just a tiny bit, to destabilize the union, because I don't have what they have. Because they have so much that they didn't even ask for, things that I have been denied because I don't have a relationship with my family or a savings account or a stable home. You owe me something, even if it's just an artisanal single-origin chocolate bar or paper out of your printer.

Everyone needs a sense of belonging. Trying to fill that need outside of a family or a couple has sent me into historical and international spirals, looking for a home that doesn't mean suffocation and an independence that doesn't mean precarity. Surely there is at least a sliver where these two needs overlap.

So I go to Amsterdam, to see my friend D and to see the beguinage, one of the last in existence. I don't really like Amsterdam. It's so pretty. Prettiness makes me suspicious.

I prefer all the ugliness front and center, not swept outward into the suburbs or inward behind a sweet smile. We stuff ourselves with pancakes—mine has meat in it but is covered in a sweet syrup, and I find this obnoxious and confusing—and we go to see the spinsters.

The beguinage used to be a walled city, but now it has shrunk to a small courtyard, not noticeably different from any other old buildings, rehabilitated and repurposed, like a shut-down pencil factory or a cathedral or any other now useless thing, turned into condos for the upper classes. But it's not the wealthy who live here. This is the last of a tradition of separate neighborhoods built for single women, most of them, historically, working class. There are roses blooming and a neat little chapel in the center of the courtyard. The women who live here have mostly closed their curtains against the curious tourists.

At the end of the twelfth century, a transformation was taking place. More and more young, unmarried women were leaving the countryside to find work in the cities. These women started to organize neighborhoods, informally and haphazardly, but near the turn of the century the church began to formalize them. And what started as a few buildings here and there coalesced into separate walled communities, all through Northern Europe.

There were hundreds of these cities, with thousands of women in residence. As a woman at the time, you had basically two options: stay within the family or devote yourself to the church. Sure, you could be a sea pirate like Anne Bonny, but that option was not available to most. If you stayed within the confines of the family, you were likely to die young in pregnancy or childbirth or immediately after childbirth or, if you didn't die, to spend most of your adult life cycling through these three stages. The plague did its best to kill off most of Europe, but not even the black death had as high a body count as just old-fashioned reproduction.

There was an escape: you could give yourself to the church. You had to cut off access to your own body, and you were removed from the world to be cloistered, chaste and devotional. But the opening of the beguinages offered a third path, a way around these institutions, marriage and the church. It gave women the chance to build a life of their own choosing (within certain parameters, of course).

Sir Thomas Moore's model for utopia was an abbey. A place of contemplation and leisure, where property was held in common, where competition could give way to charity, where greed could give way to generosity, where deprivation could give way to simplicity. A place of spiritual, personal, and intellectual development, a place of friendship and camaraderie. It was essentially a secular, humanist convent, or a beguinage.

These communities provided the infrastructure on which an independent life could be built. Each beguinage was different, depending on the country and whether it was sponsored by church or state, but the setup was often the same. There were communal domestic spaces, like community kitchens and ovens and laundries. Women could live either privately or communally, depending on preference and means. The rent paid by the more well-off members subsidized the needs of the poor and sick. There were others to keep one company, and there was a certain level of respectability, better than the total marginalization that greeted unmarried working women on the outside. There was a chapel, there was often a market. No men were allowed, so women were protected from physical and romantic violence. The community filled in the gaps of care and attention and meaning a family would provide. It gave women a role in society, it gave them purpose.

There were rules and standards of behavior, of course. Women were expected to dress modestly. Virginity was not required, but sex fell into a gray area. Children were not allowed; if a woman became pregnant she was often cast out for a year, just enough time to have the baby and leave it in a drawer at the fire station or out in the woods. Then she could return to the community, childless.

The neighborhoods were anarchic. Overseen by the church, yes, but self-ruled. There was no hierarchy, there was no police force, there was no ruler, there was only communion. And the women worked. Most worked in textile factories spinning thread, hence the word "spinster." Others were nurses, working in hospitals and orphanages. In rural areas, the beguinages, like certain convents, raised livestock and made foodstuffs like cheese and beer.

Families often did not like the beguinages. The women who lived there were ridiculed in the churches and in the town square as being unfit for marriage, as being wily and unruly and feral. They were unnaturally manly, it was said. In Walter Simon's history of the beguinage, *Cities of Ladies*, he writes about "a Middle Dutch satirical sketch of urban life, written about 1325, depict[ing] women textile workers of Brussels hanging about the street and verbally harassing male passersby with sly double entendres. After tricking the men into giving them money and drinks, the rambunctious women run off to go ice skating on the canals."

I so want a cadre of foul-mouthed, hard-drinking, ice-skating women friends to harass men on the street with me. I want to return home after a long day of work and share a meal with a city of ladies, before I retreat to my room to work on the philosophical treatise I'm writing in my spare time. Beguinages gave us philosophers, writers, theologians, women freed from the burdensome cycles and hormonal wash of pregnancy, birth, child-rearing, pregnancy, birth, child-rearing, never ceasing till one of those stages proves fatal. It's hard to become a composer when you are dead at twenty-two from birthing your fourth child.

While ridiculed for housing women no one wanted, the beguinages were often filled with women eager to escape marriage. Other women saved up money to buy spaces in the cities for their friends and family members, helping them escape the family too. In their wills, some residents left their spots in the neighborhoods to nieces, perhaps anticipating that that surly one won't make it in compulsory heterosexuality, she might need a place to crash.

The beguines were not independent. They were, like all of us, deeply interdependent. The romance of the independent life is mostly a lie. Freedom is fetishized in America, but mostly what people mean when they say they want to be free is they want to be relieved from the obligation of taking care of other people. But it is stitching ourselves together, creating complex textiles of connection and exchange, that offers us the greatest opportunities for true freedom. Allowed to relinquish caring for only their own brood, and instead to participate in a broader span of lives, they were not independent but they had the opportunity to become singular. To create an identity outside of the narrow family role of wife, mother, daughter, to create a more expansive role within a society.

The beguinages were shut down. Not for lack of interest, but because the Protestant revolution, alongside the beginning stages of industrialization, strengthened and hardened the importance of the family, mostly as a way to control capital. Northern Europe was taken over by Lutherans and Calvinists, and they had no place for women outside of the family. The beguines were sent back to their neat little family homes, and sometimes to their deaths. But a few little pockets remained, including this much reduced one in Amsterdam.

I was staying with D, who is also a spinster, living far from home. She decided to leave when her nation started to splinter and her writing against its nationalist turn made her a target.

Her boyfriend did not come with her, nor could he understand why she couldn't just tone down her rhetoric. She tells me this late at night, after dinner with a young admirer of hers. She is a tremendous force in European literature, and on most of our encounters I see her trailed by some wide-eyed young man who wants to sit at her feet but also to puff himself up. These men don't like feeling diminished in her presence; they are always trying to prove something.

"I'm reading Karl Ove Knausgaard, have you read him?"

"No," she plays dumb in her Balkan deadpan. "Who is that?"

The second she ushers him out of her apartment, after his lengthy explanation of what Knausgaard's books are like and his opinion about each and the varying assessments of respected critics, she turns to me to say, "I find Knausgaard obscene."

The conversation turns from a young man's opinions on European literature to loneliness. Despite finding satisfaction and community through work, living alone in a city in a foreign language and context, with peers mostly concerned with their own kin, it's hard to find emotional stability. Friends are often coded as the lowest priority in a person's emotional life, way below children and spouse. And once you reach a certain age, an age I reached long ago, it feels like everyone but you has children and a spouse.

Even if D doesn't feel as though her former boyfriend's decision not to join her in exile was an abandonment, I can't help but think of his inability to support her in writing what she needed to write as a kind of political abandonment. A refusal to understand why someone feels compelled and required to say hard things in difficult times, to speak out, make noise, be visible instead of melting into a silent mass, is a refusal to extend compassion. It makes me think of the Rosenstrasse protests in Berlin, not too far from where I used to live. In Berlin, during the war, intermarried couples, Aryan and Jewish, were protected by law. Until one day in 1943, when the Jewish halves of the couples were rounded up, and their Aryan spouses were pressured to file for divorce.

A group of around two hundred Aryan women showed up outside the building where their husbands were being held before deportation, and they refused to leave, despite the February cold, despite the guns being pointed at them. They stood in front of that building all day and all night, only ducking underground during air raids. Then, a week later, with no fanfare whatsoever, the doors to the holding facility opened and their husbands were returned to them.

It's heartwarming, isn't it? To think of women putting their lives on the line to save the men they love. It's a good story, but I always want to interfere with a good story, get in its way, break its narrative spine. When the pressure from the German government to separate intermarried couples began, when Jewish spouses were discriminated against and forbidden to work, when their rations were slashed, more men than women divorced and abandoned their vulnerable spouses. Those women and some of their children, now unprotected by Aryan blood, were rounded up and deported. The women of Rosenstrasse, then, were putting their bodies in the cold, in front of automatic weapons, for men who, if the tables were turned, were statistically more likely to just let them die.

But there's another story under that one. This was the only mass protest by Aryans over Jewish deportation in Berlin. People did not stand out in the cold when their friends, their colleagues, their exes, their neighbors were suddenly taken away. No one staged a mass protest when the unmarried were rounded up. People did not take to the streets when they heard of strangers disappearing in the middle of the night. No one stood outside the holding facility and demanded, "Give me back that guy who works at the grocery store, who I talk to once a week, and who gave me an extra soup bone for my dog that one time." Those people are always seen as being someone else's responsibility—let their family or lover worry about them. And if they don't have any of those, well, maybe that just shows they're not worth worrying about, full stop.

I dream of living in a beguinage with my friends, but I am ill suited to the commune. I proposed to my friend Corinna one night. There was something about that evening, everything made all fuzzy by the cocktails we were drinking and the man at the next table's generous sharing of his cigarettes, in a city where you could blessedly smoke inside the bar. The young men next to us were German, rowdy and pleasing, and our table kind of merged with theirs. The music was good, the gin was good. And there was something about the way Corinna looked, with the setting sun vibrantly accenting the volcanic cloud of red curls haloing her head.

I met her in Berlin when I was looking for a German tutor. She would smoke through our lessons, and as I struggled through the genders and tenses, she would admonish me in her East German accent, "No, that is not very good." We became close, going to the opera together or taking walks through the city. I would cook her elaborate meals, delicately planned around the food she was eliminating from her diet this week as she tried to identify a source of her hideous migraines.

So that night, filled with love and about to leave the city with no idea when I might return, I told her I loved her, and then I asked her to marry me. "Sure," she said. We exchanged the rings we had on our fingers, but they only fit on the middle fingers of our left hands. We celebrated with another round of drinks and by asking for more cigarettes, which were granted to us.

As we got up to leave, the handsome young German man who had let us smoke his stash stood, hugged me intensely, and said into my ear, as if he were dispensing great wisdom, "Don't read Phillip Roth novels."

"I know," I said.

"It's just that you look like you might. And they are bad, they are very bad for women."

"I know."

But even with my deep love for Corinna and completely sincere desire for us to stay in each other's lives until we are dead, staying at her apartment on my next trip into the city turned into a disaster. I needed a place, and she happened to have a spare bedroom in one of those rollicking apartments I long to be a part of and then fall apart in when I try. There was a constant coming and going, people crashing and people fucking and people watching *Ru Paul Drag Race* in the kitchen. A woman would wander into my room without much warning and start to argue with something I wrote about trauma and femininity. I would walk into the hallway and find people planning a feminist porn shoot. In the other room, there'd be someone making posters for an protest against the Garzweiler mine. "Can I borrow this jacket? We are going to block the train tracks to the coal mines, it is going to rain, and I don't have anything waterproof."

I can't stand being seen by another person. I would wait at my bedroom door listening for signs that I could slip into the kitchen to grab food or make a cup of tea before rushing back to the protection of my own space. Running into someone unexpectedly, having to get out of my own head and do something friendly with my face, is a weird agony for me. Some people simply have odd temperaments. Some people are just bad at being people.

So communes are basically my idea of hell, although I long to belong somewhere. If I can't manage being in an apartment with the sweetest and smartest teachers, musicians, porn directors, and bartenders I've ever met, there is no way I am going to survive living off the land with anybody who wants to live off the land. The communes of the 1960s and '70s, some of them built by lesbian separatists, were experiments in reshaping society. How do we not exploit and disassociate from nature, how do we find a more balanced way to live? But building on a reaction against the larger conservative Christian society's decree that you should save your love and body for one person only, a bunch of people decided to make loving and sharing your body with everyone compulsory. What a nightmare.

That was the seed of destruction planted in most of the radical utopian projects of the nineteenth century. There were many throughout Kansas. The land had just been ethnically cleansed through the genocide of the Native tribes, and any such landscape perceived by a person with a colonialist mindset will always look empty. Empty and ready for building whatever grand scheme you have in mind. As a result, the Midwest was cluttered with utopia, from New Harmony in Indiana to

Octagon City in Kansas to the Amana Colonies in Iowa. Most were socialist, many believed in the destruction of the nuclear family, and in quite a few the founder and ruler would decide for you who you would sleep with. You know, for the good of the culture. In some, celibacy was compulsory, in others, free love was compulsory. In many, sleeping with the founder was compulsory.

There was a belief that the ideal society would be created by forcing members to conform to what was believed to be ideal behavior. In Octagon City, a vegetarian diet was strictly enforced. In Amana, marriage was discouraged among residents, and marrying an outsider would lead to your immediate expulsion. Some utopian communities were completely atheist. Some had only communal spaces, and the need for privacy was seen as selfish.

Radical socialists believed there would be no true equality without the destruction of the biological family. Children's loyalty was to be, instead, to the community or the state. So they separated children from parents. This was a common complaint in communes and kibbutzes, that they tried to break the familial bond by keeping children away from their parents except for a few hours during the day. But it seems to me the goal should be building new bonds, not destroying old ones. Attempts to control behavior and relationships and sex generally led to the same result: believers balked at the restrictions, and many of these projects fell apart after only a few years. I'm sure some of it was also just waiting forever to be let into the bathroom or being yelled at when you've been in the shower for only a minute or two.

There were other problems. A major one being, if you are socialized into a particular belief or behavior, can you override that simply by deciding to? Fourierist communities were explicitly started to liberate women from domestic duties. Charles Fourier was a utopian thinker, lovingly bonkers, and nothing vexed him quite like the subservient position of women in the early nineteenth century. He believed that, once liberated, women might show themselves the equals or superiors of men. "We catch a glimpse," he wrote in the essay "The Oppression of Women," "of the destiny of the weaker sex, and of those powers of mind which it will exercise with complete success, as soon as it shall be restored to its natural position, which is not that of the *servant*, but of the *rival* of man; not that of attending to petty or menial domestic labors, but of confounding, as they will in association, the idle doctrines of the philosophers and moralists in defense of incoherent industry, the isolated household and the degradation of women." The quickest route to liberation was to remove the woman from the private home and from marriage, both of which were also believed to be degrading and suffocating to men. Yet in these communities, where domestic work was supposed to be shared equally by all, women reported that the communal kitchens and laundries and childcare centers were worked almost exclusively by women.

Fourier mourned society's lost contributions. How much better the world would be, he thought, if women were allowed to create philosophies, pursue artistic ambitions, voice their opinions, share their ideas. Even now, as women are creating public selves and participating in the world, even if often their philosophies read like the philosophies of men, they still volunteer for domestic confinement. And we still mourn society's lost contributions. Imagine what could be created if members of certain communities didn't have to spend so much energy calculating threats as they walked down the streets, if we didn't have to toil meaninglessly at demeaning jobs, if we weren't burdened by the inheritance of our parents' unlived lives. What songs we would hear, what buildings would be built, what words would we read if we weren't all speaking constantly the language of money and respectability.

But here is the most common problem with utopia: what do we do with the assholes? Let's reject the softheaded belief that it is always circumstance and the nurture half of the equation that creates assholes and that we can rid ourselves of them if we reorganize the world correctly. That we won't always have people among us who need sometimes to be separated out, for their good as much as our own. We can do our best to create fulfilling, peaceful, nurturing childhoods for all, removing abuse, neglect, and poverty from the realm of variables, yet there will most likely always be some glitch in the code, some anomalous figure of violence and spite to deal with.

Our current mode of banishment and containment does not help anything. Mass incarceration and the removal of the criminal from our sight has not halted the creation of new criminals. Surprisingly, traumatizing those who have transgressed through punishment and vengeance does not help rehabilitate them and make productive members of society.

But I don't want a quiet, homogeneous utopia. My perfect city is not one where everyone dresses the same, believes in the same things, lives lives indistinguishable from one another. I do not want the great noise of the world reduced and diminished to one reedy chord. The only utopia worth building is one that reintegrates everyone who has been out on the margins: the queers, the fuckups, the angry, the unlovable, the old, the ill, the misfits, and the losers. Imagine everyone who has been shipped off, from the inconvenient grandmother to the mentally ill child, the self-destructive addict to the destructive abuser, dropped off on Main Street and forcibly reintegrated into the town. Think of the reorganization of care and attention and time it would take to bring them back in. Think of the commitment it would take to ensure they could live with dignity. Think of the conversations and negotiations it would require to guarantee that a small part of the population was not burdened with all of the caretaking. Think of how we'd have to reimagine where people in need should live, and in what conditions. That, to me, is a beautiful opportunity.

What is harder to imagine is what everyone inconvenient to our comfort and our freedom could contribute, because we have lived without them for so long. Over time, we have come to believe that anyone who lives in an extreme physical or mental reality, whether institutionalized or locked away at home as a private burden, can only ever be a drain, never a resource. That belief creates and reinforces its own reality.

One reason the beguinages survived much longer than the socialist utopias seems to be that they were grounded in a genuine need, not in political idealism. They weren't trying to transform society, necessarily; they were trying to help women survive it. They were invested in the project in a way that a guy from Brooklyn dabbling in the idea that having three wives on a farm in the Catskills might be cool can never be. The Catholic Church sponsored these cities out of a charitable recognition of need, yes, but also because it knew the risks women took with their bodies and their souls within marriage and the family. Marriage for Catholics was barely one step above damnation—"better to marry than burn," and all that. But with housing crises in almost every major American city, loneliness an epidemic, a flush of diseases of despair, and suicide rates spiking—particularly through the Midwest and the Rust Belt—we have a genuine need for new ways of structuring homes and belonging, now without a powerful and wealthy institution like the church able or willing to meet those needs.

There is another unfortunate reality: need is not enough. In the late 1980s, facing hostility and violence from the world around them, a group of women decided to form a collective neighborhood by occupying and buying houses between 25th and 31st Streets and Gillham and Troost in the Midtown neighborhood of Kansas City. They called it Womantown. It was just a short walk from where my house would be, near 40th and Troost, and I could stand outside Womantown like I stood outside the beguinage, with one crucial difference. Womantown peaked with about a hundred lesbians settling into the houses, but it broke up as a formal project after only a few years. There's nothing to mark it, and no visible trace remains.

In this quiet, residential neighborhood, in early twentieth-century houses with surprising Art Deco details, a group of women tried to recreate the utopian project so many others have struggled with. They formed a community by removing fences between individual backyards, instilling open door policies, sharing domestic labor, and coming together regularly for meals and meetings.

There was certainly a need for something like Womantown. Kansas City in the '80s was cosmopolitan, but it was tainted by the conservative nature of the region. The growing AIDS crisis made the gay community freshly visible. The visibility assisted in gays' fight for acceptance, but it also made them targets for hate. That hate would formalize itself in the early '90s into the nearby Westboro Baptist Church, which made it its mission to let the world know that God Hates Fags by picketing Tori Amos concerts, Gulf War vets' funerals, and other random gatherings.

Womantown was a way of taking care of each other in a world that mostly wanted them dead.

It fell apart in possibly predictable ways. An interracial couple faced discrimination and disapproval from the other members of Womantown, which splintered solidarity. Racism was a common complaint within the gay community, as in all of Kansas City. People interpreted having a voice as having control. The domineering, certain about what was acceptable behavior and what was not acceptable behavior, tried to wrest control of the project. It's hard to say what exactly pushed things over into collapse—like much of queer history outside of the major coastal cities, it has been underdocumented and underresearched—but by the late '90s, the commune was gone and the area was returned from community to neighborhood.

And as the decade progressed and discrimination lessened, it became more difficult to sustain these parallel spaces. Marginalization often pushes people to create their own bars, churches, bookstores, and neighborhoods, but once the threat is no longer critical, it becomes easier to assimilate into the mass than to continue standing out. It's no wonder, then, that after the worst of the AIDS crisis passed, marriage equality became the rallying cry for the gay rights movement. It's easier to ask for tolerance than acceptance. It's also easier to think of yourself as an individual, rather than part of a group, when your identification with that particular demographic is not daily reinforced by others' condemnation.

Are all such projects doomed? Is the American definition of freedom—"I don't owe anybody anything, not taxes, not attention, not care"—too deeply embedded in us? Our consumerist culture has poisoned even our imaginations. When we come home exhausted from work, scrolling through Grubhub or eating Cheerios over the sink, we don't dream of a shared kitchen in the courtyard, where we can grab a bowl of freshly made soup and some bread and commiserate with others. We just fantasize about being able to afford paying someone to make those things for us. As with the Fourierist men, who believed in gender equality yet couldn't bring themselves to pick up a mop, I wonder if idealism is enough to fight off decades of socialization.

As Simone Weil writes in *The Need for Roots*, her treatise on what gives people a sense of belonging, "The notion of obligations comes before that of rights." Before we can think of what is owed to us, we must think of what we owe to each other. Otherwise we all stand there, hands out, indignant, no one willing to satisfy the needs of anyone else until they themselves have been satisfied.

It is simple and obvious, yet it goes entirely against the way we think today. This is particularly true for groups that have found themselves in decades-long fights for equality. These struggles are fueled by recitations of damage, by reminding people again and again of what has been done to the group's members, what has been kept from them, and what they are owed. A victim mentality tells us we need protection, and the best form of protection is control. The oppressed become oppressors real quick, which is how an interracial romance becomes a flashpoint in a supposed feminist utopia.

But to move past the traditional idea of the family, which tells you who you should care for and who is not worth it, takes more than just replacing "people who share my genetic makeup" or "people who are collected under this physical and economic roof" with "people who share this specific identifying marker," be it sexuality or race or gender or income status.

The idea of community is not enough. It's too floppy a concept, too nostalgic and indistinct. It doesn't just mean knitting circles and someone to bring you groceries when you're sick. It means clusters of like-minded people who shut out any dissent. Neo-Nazis have a great sense of community, as do anti-vaxxers and militias. What we need is society.

Gotta hang this
bone out to dry

Yet, after all, let us acknowledge it wiser, if not more saga-cious, to follow out one's daydream to its natural consum-mation, although, if the vision have been worth having, it is certain never to be consummated otherwise than by a failure. And what of that! Its airiest fragments, impalpable as they may be, will possess a value that lurks not in the most pon-derous realities of any practical scheme. They are not the rubbish of the mind. Whatever else I may repent of, therefore, let it be reckoned neither among my sin nor follies, that I once had faith and force enough to form generous hopes of the world's destiny—yes!—and to do what in me lay for their accomplishment.

NATHANIEL HAWTHORNE

I have traversed a treacherous sea of horrors to be with you here tonight.

AXL ROSE

I TOOK THE TRAIN from Kansas City to Chicago to see a witch. I needed her to work a spell for me, as I had given up on the real world getting the job done. She lives in an old haunted hotel near the lake, where she reads cards and tea leaves while also creating artwork for world-famous rock n roll bands.

It was a love spell I wanted, of course. That is the usual rea-son for seeking out a witch, other than wanting your president dead. After moving to Kansas City in part to get away from a married man, I had fallen for another married man. I had started the affair thinking the fact that he was polyamorous and open about his other relationships would make a difference. It didn't. I used to think the going-for-married-men thing was a matter of low self-esteem. Then late one night in a conversation with a friend who had also spent ten years as mistress to various married men, we realized we had picked up this habit at the same point: coming out of an abusive relationship. Once you've been knocked around a bit, or screamed at and humiliated in public places, or stalked, or trapped in a car with someone who isn't sure whether he should be pointing that gun at himself or at you, the full attention of a man in love can seem too dangerous. Better to deflect it a bit, get another body in there to hide behind at times.

But finally I was done with it, and I wanted these men out of my life. It had not surprised me when I came back to Kansas City that everyone I met, even people in their early and mid-twenties, was married. For many of my classmates, wedding invitations had quickly followed high school graduation invitations. There's little pressure to establish a career in the Midwestern family, particularly with so many of us cemented in our daddy's hand-me-down shoes, but the pressure to marry and birth a new generation is immense.

What I was surprised by was how many of these married couples were in open relationships, and how many of those married men wanted me to meet their wives. There was an elaborate web of overlapping marriages: this man had his own marriage but was also involved in this other person's marriage through a poly relationship with the wife, who was also connected to this other marriage over here by being the tertiary partner of this open relationship. It was like an intimate community of care, but the secret password to get in was desire. Everyone detailed their entanglements on their Tinder profiles—married to X, committed to Y, seeking fun (or more!) with you. From the inside, it probably felt great. Cozy. From the outside, it was a bit like walking past a nice bar, full of attractive people well lit with candlelight, while you accumulate wet in the rain, too poor to come in and warm yourself with a whiskey.

Clearly the message that marriage was sexually, emotionally, financially, ambitiously stifling had hit the Midwest, but these couples had made the same mistake as the rest of the country: thinking they could fuck their way out of the problem. It came from the consumerist instinct, which tries to solve dissatisfaction by adding more of the same. Are your electronic devices interrupting your sleep, driving you to distraction, preventing you from being fully present in the company of others? Try adding these new and improved electronics to your household! Is marriage making you feel trapped and bored? Try adding more people to your marriage!

I somehow fell into this web, via a socialist with a mustache and a rose tattoo. After a couple months it was clear being the mistress in an open marriage is almost exactly the same as being the mistress in a "closed" marriage. You are always aware of your place in the hierarchy. I texted the socialist at 5 a.m., a few hours after an intensely warm and happy rendezvous, that I did not think we should see each other ever again, and then I made an appointment with the witch.

Katelan is dramatically beautiful, and she opens the door to my weak and demoralized knock wearing catty eyeliner and red lips and vintage lingerie and a dressing gown. Her smile is enormous, cracking her face almost in two. I had known her for a while before I asked for her assistance, and we could talk forever about how gentrification affects the soul of the land or gripe about the Instagram girls who think being a witch is a matter of posting pictures of a tarot card next to an enormous amethyst with a lit candle and a cat in the background. (If you have never made a love interest consume your menstrual blood, you are not a real witch.) I appreciated that she knew one of the primary tasks of the witch is to tend to the dead, which I know something about too.

She had been preparing for the spell before my arrival, and she had all kinds of herbs, flowers, candles, and tarot cards set up. We sat on the floor and she poured us an infusion of rose petals and cornflowers. She asked me to write down what I wanted in a partner. "Be specific," she warned me. "The spirits like to pay tricks. If you don't write down 'unmarried,' they are definitely going to make you fall in love with someone else's husband again." I hurriedly added "unmarried" to my list. Unmarried, intelligent, warm, present, talkative, funny. "If you want him to be rich, I can add some jezebel root." I told her that I had yet to meet a rich man I wanted to talk to for longer than ten minutes, so she left it out.

"Now, very important." She got out a wedding cake candle, with a cute little groom and a cute little bride in white holding hands. "You can tell me if this is too much. If you're really just looking for something casual, we can use a normal candle. But if you're looking for a life partner, we'll use this."

I was afraid of bringing something transitory into my life again. I was repulsed by the idea of getting married, but I was sure I could control the magic, make the wedding symbolism metaphorical and not literal. "It's fine," I told her.

We mixed together the flowers and the herbs and poured them into a jar of honey. She carved a hole into the bottom of the wedding candle and placed inside it my list of requests. She lit it as well as four red candles, placed them in a circle, and sprinkled rose buds and holy oil around them. We held hands and chanted, and she talked me through a visualization. I pulled a tarot card, the Wheel of Fortune. The red candles sputtered. "That's good, they are talking to the spirits, telling them what you want." As the married couple melted and dripped, we looked for shapes in the wax to foretell what this relationship would be like. It was all phalluses and heart shapes. "A lot of good sex and love, that's a really good sign."

We sat there for hours, until everything had burned down and the tea had worn off. In the moment, I believed fully in the possibility of love and in my chances of experiencing a reciprocated version of it. As soon as I left her apartment, I started to doubt. I started to walk the few blocks back to my rented room, and as I got maybe ten meters down the sidewalk, the sky opened up and released rain, lightning, and hail. I ran. There had not been a storm in the forecast as far as I knew, and I was caught without protection.

When I finally made it back indoors, soaking wet and breathing hard, I looked at my phone. There was a text from Katelan. "A storm is a very good sign! It means the heavens heard us!" I wondered if I could hope for this.

Four months later I was married.

Between the spell and its manifestation, whenever I passed the newspaper rack outside the grocery store, a series of news stories kept catching my attention. The *Kansas City Star* had done some digging and found that over a ten-year period more than a thousand fifteen-year-old girls had been married in Missouri, most from out of state, and a third of them to considerably older men. I was living in a state with unusually lax laws on consent and marriage, where a girl of fifteen only needed the signature of one parent or guardian to marry. They didn't need to involve a judge like in other states—a judge who might notice that a teenage girl was being married off to a fifty-year-old man, as some of them were. A judge who might ask if the man had slept with his bride already, and if he had, would have known this should be considered rape. It would have been, in Missouri, although not if the pair were married.

The newspaper's website had the audio of a father explaining to a judge why he had dragged his daughter across state lines to marry her off half-willingly to a man twice her age. She was pregnant, he said. Whatever he might think of the man who had, according to the law, raped his teenage daughter, the greater tragedy and the larger concern was the possibility of a child being born out of wedlock. Legally tying his daughter to her rapist was a way to, if not sanctify the violation, then at least legitimize it.

There's a lot of outrage about this story in the news and online. A feminist commentator is horrified at the report of girls forced into commitments to men who "took advantage." Marriage should be about love, it is said, as if the history of marriage wasn't an exact replication of these stories: the father sexually guarding his daughter, handing her off to another man like property in order to protect—or elevate—the family's station.

But I curdle at the word *rape*. This story of these fifteen-year-old girls is swallowed up by the larger American story of teenage girls, one headline after another. Teenage girls sexually abused by their coach. Teenage girls sexually pursued by an adult politician. Teenage girls raped and recorded on phones by their schoolmates, the videos passed around social media.

People, and the law, who want to act as advocates twist the story in order to control it. These are not teenage girls anymore. Now they are referred to as children. The women are merely victims of these relationships, not participants. The men

73

become monsters, predators, pedophiles. Women take to Twitter, posting photos of themselves as teenagers to prove girls are not women and cannot be sexualized. The photos show awkward, metal-filled smiles, gangly poses, terrible clothing and hair choices. They are dorky and adorable, virginal and clean. There are cries to protect these girls by making laws regarding sexuality and consent stricter and more punitive, and prosecuting to the fullest extent of the law any man who violates them.

I don't recognize myself in this new version of the story. At fifteen, yes, I was an awkward nightmare of curly hair and bad skin with an attraction to shiny synthetic fabrics. I was also overwhelmed by dark, masochistic sexual fantasies, of being forcibly taken and torn apart by multiple men. It was my way of dealing with the violence of desire and whatever black hole started to suck me in when the Pianalto murder revealed the intertwining of love and death. If sex was ultimately about annihilation, then annihilate me. Perhaps the only thing that saved me was that I was too ugly to sex-murder.

A fifteen-year-old girl with a sexually jealous protective father who cares more about keeping his daughter sexually intact than emotionally intact might run into the embrace of an older man who will ram it into her. She might eroticize the violation that is already happening at home as a way of psychologically surviving it. What girls like us need is not more paternalistic protection. We don't need to be guarded from consensual, if fucked-up, sexual experiences by the police state. Nor from the violence we experience and dole out in romantic and familial relationships, nor from sexual harm. Bringing men with guns into intimate spaces has never done a moment of good.

What we need are better outlets. We need a culture that isn't super conflicted about whether we are innocent babies or dirty Lolitas who want it bad. We need partners who don't joyfully respond to a limping gazelle routine by pretending to be lions. We need spaces where we can be degraded only to the extent we choose, partners who aren't so willing to drag us into the underworld. And when those outlets prove to be destructive, we need an easy way out, which means material resources like housing, transportation, and counseling must be readily available. If the broken and vulnerable girl is a problem, someone to be protected and controlled, maybe we should manufacture fewer of them in our families, schools, and churches. But also, if the predatory man is a problem, someone to be surveilled and controlled, maybe we should create fewer of them through abuse, neglect, and emotional murder.

On late-night talk shows the comedians keep showing videos and images of the president putting his hands all over his adult daughter, and they laugh and they laugh. So gross and weird, they all agree, as if it's an anomaly. The images remind me of the purity balls on the evangelical side of my family. At father-daughter dances, the awkward girls wear floofy white polyester dresses, like a dry run for their future weddings to guys who will closely resemble their own fathers. But until that day, each is making a pledge of sexual purity to her dad. Then her dad, making a pledge to sexually protect her, he puts his hands on his daughter's waist and a chastity ring on her finger, and they slow dance, like lovers, and the old hysterical rumblings of my stomach start up again. I want to vomit, I want to scream.

When I was fifteen, this guy in my class was always wearing the same Guns N' Roses T-shirt. "I Used to Love Her," it read, a photo of a young naked blonde, cut into pieces, her very hot body dismembered and disconnected. "But I had to kill her" was the rest of the line of that song, just one in a long line of songs by men about killing the ones they loved. Johnny Cash,

Eminem, Garth Brooks, the Rolling Stones, Nick Cave, all leering over us while explaining how Thanatos is doing a dance with Eros and their desire to love us is entwined with their desire to kill us. And we're all just sitting there saying, "Oh. Okay."

I remember teachers studying that Guns N' Roses shirt, looking for a nipple or an ass crack among the strewn body parts, something that would make it officially obscene so they could force him to stop wearing it. I didn't know that song, but I had taped "November Rain" off the radio, and I would listen to it over and over again, replaying in my head the music video, the one where Axl Rose is getting married to a woman and then all of a sudden she is in a casket.

The guitar solo, the second one, in that song is still entwined with the prairie. It is the sound of hanging your head out of the rear window at night as your friend speeds down the interstate, as the dark wheat fields blur past you and an endless display of stars stands still and eternal above you.

My friend Missy had introduced me to metal. Also professional wrestling and hairspray. She taught me how to heat up the cheap pencil eyeliner with a cigarette lighter to get a better smudge. We'd go over to her place to swap Stephen King paperbacks and watch Bret the Hitman Hart and Randy Savage and Ric Flair play-fight. In my home, television was forbidden. In hers, it was rarely turned off, and we'd half watch while drawing on our jeans with Bic pens and gorging on junk food (also forbidden in my home) from the Mighty Mart.

Like everything else in my life, in the years after the Pianaltos' deaths my musical taste went dark. It wasn't just puberty and its usual way of wrecking any sunshininess within you that's managed to survive childhood. I went from Madonna and other cute little girls bopping around in music videos to trolling the few industrial and metal bins at the mall music store. I needed the noise entering my head to match the noise already filling it. With Guns N' Roses, I liked the trashy abrasiveness, but I was having a hard time finding myself in the scene. I would read interviews with Axl and Slash bragging about being in a restaurant and having girls drop to their knees and start blowing them under the table in front of everyone, and I would wonder what I was supposed to do with that information. The girls in the class ahead of me, with the big tits and the high bangs and the Guns N' Roses and AC/DC and Def Leppard T-shirts that they cut the sleeves off to turn into tank tops, also carefully enlarging the arm holes so people were sure to get a flash of bra when they moved—they bragged about their blow-job skills, they went to every hard rock band that came to the Stiefel Theater in the much larger town of Salina (pronounced in an aggressively white way with a long I) forty-five minutes away. By "much larger" I mean at least forty thousand people lived there. There was talk of cute roadies, sneaking backstage, even more blow jobs. I didn't feel comfortable at the shows or in the bands' shirts or in conversation with the others who lined up to buy their album on the release date.

But I did feel an affinity for Axl. Not the swaggering, boastful Axl. Nor the soulful, "I could be your boyfriend as I sing this song about a woman whose arm I maybe broke," sweet Axl. The broken one. Axl had been ruined by Kansas too, after all. About a century before he was born, a man in Topeka started telling people that his sermons were direct messages from god and that the Holy Spirit spoke through him. When he started making nonsense sounds and writhing, that was the sign of the spirit's presence—speaking in tongues, speaking in god's language through his mortal body. Enough people believed Charles Fox

Parham that a whole new way of believing in god was invented and the Pentecostal church spread. (It turned out to be a lot like the old way of believing in god, but getting to roll around on the floor and lose control of your throat was exciting enough to make it feel like something new.)

Axl's family's life revolved around their small Indiana town's Pentecostal church. Both his church and his stepfather taught him that the world was evil and decadent. Music was forbidden, women were the source of evil going back to Eve. As usual, though, the biggest threat was not the world but his family, and he was kidnapped and held by his father, who abused and possibly molested him. His conservative church and family had no way of helping to put a traumatized soul back together.

The metal scene back then was centered in Los Angeles, so that is where he went. It was clear from the beginning that Guns N' Roses, despite sharing a spot on the radio dial with Warrant, Ratt, Poison, White Snake, and all the other Aqua Net addicts, had some substance to them. Axl wasn't making dumb innuendos about vaginas—cherry pie, sugar, meat—like all the prancing fools lip-syncing next to girls in bikinis writhing on sports cars. Under all the guitars and drums on his records there was a prettiness, in the songs and in him. That prettiness, and fragility, didn't seem like something he was altogether comfortable with.

The stories of domestic violence came out as quickly as the music. Even the women in his videos didn't fare so well. They are always raging and being raged at, shoving and being shoved. Here is his wife in a coffin, here is Slash driving a car off a cliff with a screaming woman in the passenger seat.

When you're a teenage girl, listening to and seeing all of this, you can either put yourself in the place of the woman going off the cliff, the woman on her knees under the table in a crowded restaurant, or cast yourself as the as-yet-unintroduced woman who will save the tortured genius from all this, and from himself. I instead pictured myself as Axl, not as a woman circling him. It wasn't *Appetite for Destruction*'s anthems and seventh-grade slow-dance jams that did it. I wanted to live inside the baroque nightmare of *Use Your Illusion I & II*.

There is something incredibly abrasive about these records, and listening to them is still like trying to comfort yourself by wrapping your body in barbed wire. They came out at a weird time. The early 1990s marked the handover from excess to eccentricity. It was clear Axl wanted to transition into what popular music was becoming, a more personal, less manufactured form of expression. Artificially constructed pop stars—faces and bodies sculpted by surgeons, music created by corporate teams—gave way to growling, howling monsters crawling out of the margins to sing about their alienation. The top of the charts went from Michael Jackson to Nirvana in an instant, and the whole culture shifted.

Guns N' Roses at first seemed set to manage the transition, as their music shifted from easy rockers to something more complex. Half of the cuts on *Use Your Illusion* were exhaust-choked time-wasters, but emerging between those were songs with complicated time signatures, intricate orchestration, and soul-searching lyrics.

But neither the media nor the critics gave them the space they needed to transition. The band had become a symbol for all the bloat and entitlement and greed and excess of the '80s, and *Use Your Illusion*, it wasn't even a double album, it was two albums released separately, meaning you paid more, and half the songs weren't even worth it, and the good ones, of course, were evenly distributed between the two volumes. I ended up buying each album twice, as this was also when I was switching from cassettes to CDs, and then there were the singles. All told I invested maybe fifty dollars for what was really just five songs, which, for a thirteen-year-old, was two and a half months' allowance. I wasn't the only one who felt ripped off. The albums were wildly successful but also representative of what the rest of the decade wanted not to be, manipulative and inauthentic.

And then there was the fan base. The critics had always worked themselves into fits over the rise of metal and cock rock, fanning themselves at the sight of white-trash crowds gathered to revel in the glorious guitars and those drums you can feel in your guts. Look at all those *Kansans*, with their hot rods and their distressed denim, what is even going on there?

Part of it was the usual hostility between critic and fan, the coastal elites drinking their martinis or chablis or whatever while snobbishly stamping GOOD or BAD on individual units of cultural production, versus all of these heartland mouthbreathers going to the cineplex to watch *Die Hard 15: O Death Remove Thy AR-15* anyway. "What are they even thinking," the critics ask themselves, "reading *The Da Vinci Code* despite our warnings, listening to Mötley Crüe despite our hesitations? Don't they want our guidance? Don't they believe in sophistication?" But then part of it was also clear classist buffoonery, and the knowledge that if the coastal elites tried to order their Manhattan cocktails in the heartland mouthbreathers' bar they might get a beer bottle to the back of the head.

There's a well-passed-around anecdote of critical darlings Nirvana meeting Guns N' Roses at an MTV awards show. Axl had talked trash about Kurt Cobain and Courtney Love's drug problems in a notorious *Vanity Fair* article about Love's pregnancy that had almost gotten their baby daughter Frances taken away by social services. A few weeks later, their entourages ran into each other backstage.

A spat broke out between Love and Axl's supermodel girl-friend. "Shut your woman up," Axl shouted at Kurt, a retort met only with laughter. Axl was just a few years older than Kurt, yet it may as well have been a generational divide between them. Rose stormed off, as Love yelled the purest insult she could at his retreating back: "He dates models."

If this moment could be rendered as an eight-foot-tall historical painting by some Frenchman, it would be the visual representation of the moment the '80s fully shifted into the '90s. On one side, we have the lines of cocaine, the sparkles, the phallic guitars surrounded by drooping, high-maintenance femininity with blank doe eyes. On the other, needles and spoons, ironic smirks, ironic wardrobes, ironic sincerity. In the middle stands our fallen hero, in a bandanna and billowy pirate shirt, howling. Isn't it you, my audience, who wanted me to fuck models, trash hotel rooms, and tell the publisher of *Spin* magazine to suck my fucking dick? You think you can just change your mind? Well, it did.

Axl was looking to be redeemed, not understanding that America doesn't believe in redemption. He got fat. He got self-conscious. He got plastic surgery. He recorded hundreds of hours of music but refused to let anyone hear it. He fought a war with the world and with himself, and he lost on all fronts.

There's a song on *Use Your Illusion*, "Don't Damn Me," where Axl asks of his audience both "don't damn me" and "don't hail me." Neither to glamorize his abuse and violent anger, nor to condemn him for it. "I've been where I have been and I've seen what I have seen," and who he is and how he behaves should be understood within that context.

One thing I keep thinking as I read through the story of Axl Rose is that, had I had it a little rougher, had I been socialized as a boy and encouraged to express pain outward as anger and violence rather than inward as feminine self-harm and depression, I could have ended up as the abuser rather than the abused. Because every suicidal impulse I have had in my life has been a desire to self-murder. Born not so much out of despair as out of a compulsive disgust and hatred turned inward. I want to destroy, violently, what I hate. Had I learned to hate the world to avoid hating myself, or to hurt someone else to avoid hurting myself, I don't know that I would have had the psychological integrity to resist.

Because the line in the song I keep tripping on is his assertion that he "didn't want to be a man." There had been the men of god and the men of the home, and he had been betrayed by both. In the video for "Welcome to the Jungle," it's men of power he recoils from, soldiers and police doling out violence against the vulnerable. Most of the guys I knew with Guns N' Roses T-shirts ended up in the military, some ended up in jail, some both. They didn't talk about the bruises and burns they showed up to school with either.

A former lover who was born in the wrong century once complained about the contemporary "have it all" mode of life. We go into the world expecting we will find achievement in every avenue: we will marry, we will bear children, we will have a successful career, we will be respected in society, and so on. I had been complaining about essays that were circulating, mostly written by upper-class white women moaning that they had maybe had to choose between a good home life and a good work life.

"Can Women Have It All?" the headlines screamed.

"Jesus, who'd want to?" my monkish lover asked. "Now we function like every house is a little kingdom, having to recreate the whole world for itself. And they all protect what they have and refuse to share because they think everyone else out here is covetous."

The nuns, they used to retreat from the world to pray for all us sinners, so the rest of us didn't have to. Your sister, she has the children to continue the bloodline, so you don't have to. The poet, she articulates the darkest recesses of her heart, so you don't have to. The farmer grows potatoes for everyone, so you don't have to.

We want to be "fulfilled," but that word sounds like the house of a hoarder who, not knowing what she wants, simply buys everything she comes across in the insane hope this product will be it. Do I want a grilled cheese pan, a pan made to make grilled cheese sandwiches and nothing else? Well, how could I possibly know until I have it and use it and then remember that I don't actually like grilled cheese sandwiches? Do I want to be married with children? Well, how could I possibly know until I force these people into my life and realize that actually I would rather live on a farm and grow turnips than wake up to a hungry scream emanating from down the hall one more night?

When we look at what prevents family violence, it's not intervention by the state. Arresting abusers and stalkers hasn't decreased the amount of domestic violence in America. Every day brings another story of how a social worker or state employee meant to protect a child from its own parents failed miserably, but the story less often told is how a person barely keeping it together had their situation made worse by the constant surveillance of protective services. What seems to work instead is the involvement of other people. For a woman in a marriage that has gone dark to have resources outside of the marriage, and the ability to be honest with the people around her. For a child with violent parents to have allies outside of the family. And for the person who is waging the violence to be held accountable and to have to see and say what he or she has done.

If Shirley Pianalto or either of the two girls had feared this man in their house, if they had been aware he might want them dead, they do not seem to have told anyone in town. And how could they, given the way these small towns function. Any intimation that something dark was going on inside that house would have provoked gossip, not the rallying of support. Look, if your barn falls down, people will come from all over the county to help you rebuild it, and they will bring sandwiches. If your husband tries to kill you, suddenly it is none of anybody's business, that's all I'm saying.

But constructing your family like a kingdom doesn't just make it harder for others to get in. It makes it harder for you to get out. How many people are trapped in abusive or controlling or just unsatisfying situations simply because they can't manage the world outside their home? They can't scrounge up the resources to feed, clothe, and house themselves or their children. They can't bear the thought of starting over with nothing. They look at all they will have to compete for, from work to housing to love, and their self-assessment tells them that what they have now is all they deserve. So they stay.

What could we have done for little Axl? Things might have been different had there been people in his life to show him other ways of believing in and being faithful to god, other ways of loving that are about care and not control. Someone definitely should have taken him to the opera.

Of course, the question running through my head underneath all of this is, always, how could we have kept the Pianaltos alive? I have typed out this question but I don't know how to answer it. I check the news to distract myself for a moment, and there are two stories. One is a woman who cared for her developmentally disabled child, seemingly devotedly, for years before murdering him with a gun. Another is a woman who was caring for her adult mentally ill son, who called the police when he became violent with her, and the police murdered him.

In both stories, the mother is the only real caregiver. Ostensibly there are resources like medical care, institutions and facilities, social workers. But most of those resources cost more for a month's care than the families can manage to earn. Both women tried to bring in intermediaries, to provide a little distance between themselves and their children. In one case that intermediary rejected the mother when she could no longer pay; in the other the intermediary murdered her child.

Each of their sons deserved care. Each deserved people who were devoted to him, who could meet his extraordinary needs and give him time and attention. But also, each mother deserved a network of support. Not only other family members, but an entire force of people, to stand between her and her child when she needed it. And that child deserved to have that team know the family's history, their context, their patterns of behavior, what they were and were not capable of. And all of that should have been available without a price tag. Instead all we got are a couple of dead kids.

And what do we do with the Axl that exists now? Is he canceled? Is he forever an abuser? What does rehabilitation even look like, other than admitting what you have done and trying to make amends and live a different life, which, given how difficult we make life for ex-convicts, particular for those punished for sexual offenses, doesn't seem to be enough for us. Part of the kingdom mentality is the belief that we should have the right to cast out anyone unwanted and that any experience we do not explicitly ask for should not happen to us.

Every one of us who built and supports and chooses a system that creates Axls, and fifteen-year-old girls forced into marriages to their rapists, and dead wives and daughters, and haunted, angry men—we owe it to them to keep them alive, to hold their bodies, to take care. They are our responsibility.

I didn't recognize him at first. As my Tinder date, yes, but not as the manifestation of the spell. I guess I thought it would be obvious, overwhelming even. Not something that almost didn't happen. I mean, if fate is going to come find you, it should be noisy and take up a lot of room, right? And also, clearly, for the sake of decency but also a sense of cosmic harmony, the gods should not be on Tinder. Eros should not be swiping.

Because I almost didn't show up. I almost didn't answer his Super Like and message, only being in Chicago for a couple of days anyway. Had the friend I'd been meeting before him not had somewhere else to go, had I been a little too comfortable where I was, had my last Tinder date been just slightly worse—already a pretty bad two-hour history lesson on where things had gone wrong between him and his newly ex-wife (at first he thought it was her being too demanding, but now that he's had a couple months of therapy he has learned to understand the part he played in the breaking down of the bonds between them, and oh, by the way, are you going to finish those fries)—I would have stayed at the Green Mill all night and skipped it.

I went. I had pulled the Fool as my tarot card for the day, so I figured why not. I went to the way-too-dark bar with the bartenders with the waxed mustaches and the fourteen-dollar tequila cocktail with the name that puns on how "Juan" kinda sounds like "one." I had picked the place at random by searching on my map app for cocktails within a mile of where I was standing at the time.

When he walked in the bar, there was no jolt of recognition, no "I'm going to marry that man." I thought he was handsome, I noticed he seemed startled that I was already at the bar, like maybe he thought he'd have time to prepare himself, or maybe he wanted to skulk in unseen with the opportunity to ditch before I saw him. Within minutes I was already writing the date off. Nico wouldn't make eye contact, and I guessed that was because he found me boring or unappealing. He said he had just finished his master's degree and would be returning soon to his home country of Colombia, and I was on the verge of yet again giving up all of my belongings to move from Kansas City back to Berlin. I decided I would have one more drink, then head back to my AirBnB, with a stop at a convenience store for some whiskey and potato chips. But somewhere before I reached that point, since the stakes were so low, I guess we decided to tell each other the truth.

I offered the information that I thought marriage should be abolished. He agreed, telling me how he had watched as a boy the women in his life bend and cater to his unfaithful father. I had just been in Madrid, where I had met a woman who was part of an organization that organized the mass occupation of vacant apartment buildings owned by banks. It had changed something in my thinking about how a person can and should live. She had spoken very movingly about how difficult collective action and thinking was to someone raised to think of herself as an individual, used to caring only for her own needs. How richly rewarding and exhausting moving as a group could be. And also how discouraging it was that so many women in the group often had to bargain and cajole and hector their husbands to watch the children during strikes and demonstrations. The men would often proclaim themselves communist, yet gladly rule over their little private kingdoms.

And he told me how inept he found most American activists,

who believed in protest but not direct action. And what a shock it was to immigrate during an Obama administration and find yourself living under a Trump administration. And how helpless he felt, watching his own country's political situation deteriorate in his absence. He still helped to run a nonprofit back in Bogotá, but the changing atmosphere there meant the work of the organization was becoming more and more dangerous, and he no longer knew where he should be. Soon I was on my fifth cocktail, not feeling drunk at all, just liquid, and when he suggested we go back to his place to watch a David Fincher film I said yes, as long as first I could show him the music video for "November Rain," which I had already described in excruciating detail.

Two days later I met my friend Mairead at the bar in Union Station, waiting for my train back to Kansas City, drinking an afternoon beer to help with my hangover, with an enormous hickey on my neck. "How are you?" she asked after she stopped laughing.

"I think I might be in love."

I didn't even think about the witch and that spell until nine days later, after he had proposed and I had already accepted. There had not been one big moment when I realized I wanted to spend my life with this person. Instead there was a series of little moments, like the way he bestowed sincere kindness and attention on the people around him, and how when he said he was going to do something he did it, and the way he obviously lived by the principles he believed in, and then there was his smile and the way his hair looked in the morning, all of which, when he asked, "Would you marry me?" coalesced in my head into a yes.

If this were a podcast, if this were a true-crime book, if this were a memoir, this would be the happy ending. There was the darkness, brought on by the betrayal of a protector who turned out to be a predator, but I would be healed, all these years later, having made my way through therapy and bad relationships and moments of clarity, through to the arrival of the husband. Our heroine learns to trust, and to love, again. We could show the splintered family reconciling at the wedding, with a sentimental father-daughter dance and a handshake, silent but speaking volumes, between dad and groom. A bad man makes a wound, a good man heals it. Fade out.

But, but, I think, as the hysteric rises in me once again, refusing to let anything just be pretty or neat, to get the arc right, don't we have to know how the murder happened? Shouldn't we tell the story of the Pianalto family, why Shirley was in the position she was in, the position to be murdered? Is it enough to say, oh, well, she learned about the importance of loyalty and how it was acceptable to stay in a marriage to a man you're afraid of from her mother. But, but, then, where did her mother learn it? Oh well, from her mother. And her? Soon, just to understand the story of how a man could kill the three women closest to him, we have to bring in the entire ancestral line, we have to trace the family's story all the way back through multiple generations, through centuries and eons. But, but, what about why no one said anything to her, why she didn't confide in anyone in town that her life was in danger? Ah, well, then we should put something in about how rural life goes, and how the preachers all talk about the importance of the wife being subservient, but to understand why that is, we have to go back to the Reformation, then maybe all the way back to when the patriarchal order was first established, maybe even further back then, maybe to the Big Bang, to truly understand how people kill people they love, and how we allow it to happen.

Soon it's all revealed to be a big, bloody mess. It's impossible to contain and impossible to transform all by yourself. Standing outside of it, standing inside of it, none of that actually changes the reality of all the dead women and all the broken men.

And knowing all of it, the scope of the issue and the statistics and the very real lived experience, none of that stopped me from saying "I do" to the judge under fluorescent lights in the basement room of the downtown Chicago courthouse and to the man I loved. It only fleetingly crossed my mind before the taco place we went to right after brought us our margaritas, but then the owners brought us shots of tequila to join in our celebration, and the moment passed.

It began to reemerge, however, as we started the process of establishing residency for Nico. It was clear that our whirlwind romance, which seemed dead dreamy to most, looked suspicious to the United States government. We were at a disadvantage already in establishing ourselves as a legitimate relationship with the Department of Homeland Security given our whimsically brief courtship, and our attorney made it clear we needed to present ourselves as a traditional married couple to make up the difference. There was a checklist. We would need to merge ourselves financially, we would need wedding rings and a photo album, we would need a joint credit card, we would need documentation of a shared residence. "It would help if you could buy a car," with both of our names on the title.

It will look suspicious, I'm told, if he has not met my blood family, despite my rarely seeing or speaking to them. I only told my parents I was married days later, but now, I was instructed, it would help things along if it looked like I had a normal relationship with them. Suddenly it didn't matter, all the years I had spent recreating what I was supposed to receive from them, all the familial relations I established all over the world: my "daughter" Riley in Philadelphia, my "twin brother" Christopher in Chicago, my true love Honeybee, my "wife" Corinna in Berlin, my "sister" in Istanbul. . . . When I argued that families are more complex these days, that lives are less traditional and more scattered, I was told I would be lucky to get a case worker who would have a sophisticated understanding of modern life and love. Any deviation from the norm was likely to look like a lie. It would be better, and less risky for Nico's livelihood and happiness, if I gave in. If I handed over my financial future, if I established myself in his home, if I wore the ring, if we blended families. If I locked myself into the traditional structure I had spent my lifetime trying to disassemble.

The weight of not doing this wouldn't be borne by me but by the person I loved. By refusing, I would be putting his ability to live and work in the United States at risk. There had already been issues with his visa, and he had to be fired temporarily from his workplace in order to straighten it out. I could solve all these problems, all of his problems, simply by acquiescing. There was a chance that we could go in messy and still be found legitimate in the eyes of the state, but it was hard for us to figure out how big a risk that would be. How selfish I would be to insist on my individuality.

I gave in, to all of it. I found a subletter for my place in Berlin, signed onto his lease, and moved into his apartment. We opened a bank account together. We traveled to landmarks simply so we could take our picture together in front of them. But I tried to draw the line at introducing him to my family. It became a problem.

"I want to go to Lincoln. I want to see where you are from."

"I don't want that!" I would mostly shriek, storming out of the room whenever it came up. The thought of going back there, it was like a hand on my throat. Little dots swam before my eyes.

"It'll look weird if we don't, don't you think?" He would follow me around the apartment. "It won't be that bad, because I'll be there this time."

Gather around, because the hysteric's performance is going to begin again. In fact, it has never ended. Out and up in a wail that she will use to try to clarify the urgency, the realness, but that will somehow only further discredit her. And then the guilt, because she knows this is too much, she knows this ruins everything, she knows she is only making things worse.

But at least it no longer has to be pretty. At least she does not have to pretend she doesn't see the blood on the ground anymore.

Get your
weapons ready

DAD TWO

THE CITIZEN

John Brown

HE MADE QUITE THE IMPRESSION. We were a group of school-children, on a field trip to the state capitol in Topeka for the first time, and we stopped on our tour in front of the mural of John Brown. His arms were stretched wide like Jesus, but rather than an expression of brokenness and sorrow, he radiated madness and fury. In one hand was a rifle, in the other a Bible.

"He was a great man." He was stepping over bodies.

I have such a clear memory of this mural, I must have been frightened of it. The pool of blood, the fire raging behind him, his mouth open in a yawp. Only now, thirty years later, studying this mural again, still a little frightened by it, do I notice the letters *alpha* and *omega* on the pages of the open Bible. Subtle, I think.

Did John Brown die for our sin of slavery? Did he lead us into salvation? The song "John Brown's Body" worms into my head and won't leave. I wonder when we were first taught to sing it, we must have been very young. The version I hear now is of that tuneless, bored variety, singing "glory glory hallelujah" with a lack of enthusiasm that can only be created by being told that the thing you are singing about was resolved and done with a long time ago.

There is another part of the mural, one I had never noticed before. John Brown kind of takes up all of the energy of the room. On the adjacent wall, next to a doorway, the conquistador Coronado and Father Padilla gaze over the plains. Father Padilla is referred to as the first Kansas martyr. He met his death here, working as a missionary. He was a man of peace, or so the story goes. The Natives, mysteriously and savagely, because they are mysterious and savage, decided to stone him to death, because they did not want him to leave. At least according to the non-Native people who were telling the story. But I don't know, man.

As a child, these stories are absorbed unthinkingly. John Brown, Father Padilla, martyrs of the plains. They were simply trying to civilize the masses, and they met their deaths for it.

There are specific ways a dead man becomes a hero. First, he has to stand alone. Any collaborators, teachers, partners, or family members have to be written out of the story. He can have a dutiful wife who quietly supports him, and he can have followers who do what he says, but heroes must be singular, not plural.

Second, contradictions and shittiness have to be written out. If he does something morally repugnant, based on certain criteria (e.g., raping a twelve-year-old used to be fine but now is not; raping his dutiful wife is still fine), it will have to be omitted from the story. But other bad behavior, like murder, arson, and theft, can be insisted on as morally right if it is done for the right reason.

And third, a dead man becomes a hero if the people he murders, whose homes he sets fire to, steals from, etc., are either wiped out or not given an opportunity to bear witness to their suffering. They must be discredited via association with some institutional evil (colonialism, slavery, etc.) or they must be genocidally silenced.

I wonder if the reason we were taught about Bleeding Kansas and the abolitionist movement so early and so frequently in school is because it is the only time in our state's history we were unmistakably the good guys. Before then the history of Kansas was a history of genocide and major fauna slaughter. After that, of industrialized agriculture and cryptofascist religion and politics.

But for one brief, shining moment Kansans did the right thing, and claiming their rightness via ancestral association means we no longer have to actually do anything during our lifetimes. We won't have to accept the repercussions of boldly voicing our opposition to the way things are, which might affect our business, or estrange us from family and friends, or diminish our social standing, or raise the risk of being assassinated by an extremist or executed by the state. We can reassure ourselves that we are good because, you know, our great aunt five times removed lived in a place whose government made the right call about something. And maybe she agreed with that right thing or maybe when she got drunk she called the politicians a bunch of thieves and liars, either way we are basically saints now, praise the ancestors. That sort of thing.

As Kansas moved toward statehood, the question of whether it would be a slave state or a free state dominated the political debates. The country was stuck in an idiotic stalemate, each side having the same number of states, and each side wanted the +1 to help it dominate the other in the legislature. The federal government decided, well, fuck it, let's just start this war that's been brewing already and let the residents decide what kind of state they want to live in, tip the balance, and let a bunch of people die because we can't be bothered to do the right thing.

There was propaganda, there was violence and slaughter, there was an influx of strangers claiming residence. There was ballot box stuffing, there was intimidation. So it's not like everyone in the state got together and talked things through and decided the only moral decision would be the abolition of slavery. It was that our side won, through unspeakable tactics and brute force, and now we, in our seventh-grade state history class, get to take credit for it.

It wasn't like there weren't people arguing for a bloodless transition. Men and women took to pulpits to argue against keeping human beings as property. Plays, books, and songs were written. Women formed sewing circles and passed around radical literature. People housed and fed those escaping horrific conditions. People collected money and took care of each other.

But if you search the textbooks for information about abolitionists in Kansas around the time of statehood, the name you'll typically find is John Brown. He was impatient for change, and he was less interested in raising consciousness than in laying waste. Supporters of slavery were crossing the border from Missouri and setting fires, terrorizing entire towns, and spreading violence. Something had to be done, and John Brown believed he was the only one who could do it.

Like a lot of political men, John Brown was disappointing. His business schemes kept failing. He teetered between debt, bankruptcy, and profligacy. His family lived in squalid conditions, and his children kept dying of disease. He was a violent father and husband, documenting in journals the severe physical punishment he doled out to keep the rest of his family in line.

If he couldn't make himself memorable as a captain of industry or as the beloved head of a family, he could at least perhaps make himself a remarkable political figure. The abolition of slavery was his chosen cause, although the source of his belief that the institution was immoral is unclear. Historians point to specific speakers he listened to and conversed with—Frederick Douglass and Sojourner Truth—and to the abolitionist churches he was affiliated with. But you can listen to all the persuasive speakers in the world and still sit there with your arms crossed and your mind set. What it takes to turn a person toward a particular worldview is mysterious. What is the seed from which grew the radical fruit? It wasn't that he thought all human beings were equal: his rough treatment of his family shows that. It wasn't even that he believed in racial brotherhood. To Brown, black people were pitiable figures. They needed rescue, being naturally inferior, and they required white people's assistance to civilize them.

His abolitionist views were, then, probably associative and self-serving. Most political views are. We think of our political stances as being the product of reason, but if that were true, as issues were discussed rationally in a public forum we would find more consensus than polarization. We would be swayed by debate rather than by intense feeling.

If we believe we come to our political beliefs through cool-headed, rational thought, that allows us to think that our political opponents are irrational maniacs. We came to our conclusion intellectually, so these other people, who came to the opposite conclusion, must be irrational, overly emotional, dogmatic lunatics in serious need of correction and reeducation.

Most of us, however, inherit our politics. We either admire our parents and the lives they have made for themselves, and take on their viewpoints as our own, or we manage our disappointment in them and the choices they have made through a stance of extreme opposition. Or we hear a celebrity's or a pop star's political take and decide to buy it alongside their branded T-shirts. Or we want to bed someone, so we find ourselves suspiciously open to their ideas. Or we want to gain entry to a social circle, so we associate ourselves with its beliefs. Or we see a power vacuum in a movement and, unable to find respect or validation in our daily life, storm in there and insist on being followed. Or we mistake fervor for conviction and intuitive leaps for logic.

When asked to define what we believe, we start with our affiliations. I'm a feminist. I'm a Republican. I'm Evangelical. I'm in the DSA. Maybe we think of this as shorthand, a way of summing up our beliefs, but often we choose our affiliations first, and the adoption of political belief flows from there. We want to associate ourselves with a movement or a value or a tradition, rather than work to figure out what we value and how best to express that value in action or representation.

"I would never vote for a Democrat." I heard that a lot in Kansas, the reddest of the reds. Never mind that Kansas has had several Democratic governors and representatives and state officials. When it came to the presidential election, the ultimate us-versus-them election, the time to pick who we choose to affiliate ourselves with on a national stage, it had to be a Republican. This wasn't because there was no middle ground, no shared perspective on at least some issues. It was because it was about how we wanted to be represented. And what the Democrats represented—rather than believed in—was too . . . soft. Wishy-washy. Bleeding heart. Liberal. Emotional. Tax rates and foreign policy and immigration reform mattered less than association and representation.

What Kansans are, instead, is traditional. Conservative. God-fearing. Industrious. And they prove that by voting to eradicate social welfare programs, so that when they succeed it is clear they deserved every bit of it. They prove that by electing fine Christian men who have good standing in their communities and their churches, and they don't allow what those men do at home to sway their opinion.

The attempt to associate themselves with the "right side" of the Civil War extends beyond the crazy John Brown mural in the capitol. The entire Republican party calls itself the "party of Lincoln" now, as if he were still there, running the GOP strategy, his head never blown off by a man who traveled far to witness Brown's execution personally.

What are the ideas we have inherited from John Brown? When we talk about heritage, when we talk about pride, what are we saying we've learned from him? Is it that all humans are equal? Not even he believed that, and if that were what we'd learned, LGBTQ people would be protected by state antidiscrimination laws, and sexual contact between two people of the same sex wouldn't still be illegal as of 2019. Is it a legacy of antiracist action? The state has a long history of Klansmen, white nationalists, and anti-immigration sentiment. So why do we cling to this image? Why do we bring the Civil War up again and again, as if the position taken by a political party or a single individual more than 150 years ago says anything about who we are today?

Kansas does live in the lineage of John Brown, but for a different reason than what is claimed. His influence is felt in this state in the persistent belief that if you are certain about an issue, and if you believe yourself to be righteous, you are permitted to attempt to reshape the world with violence and bloodshed. All you need to live out god's plan is a gun.

It was the Summer of Mercy. A year after Mr. Pianalto murdered his family and himself, a group calling itself Operation Rescue set up camp outside a medical facility in Wichita, Kansas. Wichita was the big city for us, mostly because it had an airport, which no one in my family ever used, and it had two shopping malls—with multiple floors! It had a Toys "R" Us. It was hours away by car, but the influence of the protests found its way to Lincoln, where I lived.

Suddenly our Sunday school class stopped teaching about the Good Samaritan or Jesus's benevolence. Our teacher started showing us videos of exorcisms, even though we were Methodist and I'm not sure Methodists even believe in that sort of thing, and lecturing us on the sins of homosexuality and abortion. AIDS was a curse, god's punishment for the unnatural unholiness of the gay community. Abortion was murder. Billboards started going up on the interstate with Bible verses telling us that god knew us and loved us even in the womb.

It wasn't the first time there were anti-abortion protesters in the city. Operation Rescue and domestic terrorists had been targeting Kansas for years, making it an ideological battleground for the abortion debate. Abortion had been considered a closed subject for a while, contested only in mellow protests by a mostly Catholic pro-life opposition that had grown out of a religious objection to the Vietnam War. Every life counted and deserved the opportunity to flourish; that included drafted soldiers, the Vietnamese, those incarcerated on death row, and the unborn.

But in the 1980s and '90s protests were taken over by an Evangelical community that found itself at odds with an increasingly permissive secular culture. ACT UP and third-wave feminism created greater cultural visibility for the sexualities, lifestyles, and genders these conservative Christians found abhorrent. Homosexuality was on Broadway, it was winning Oscars. (Or rather, straight men playing gay men were winning

Oscars. The distinction was lost.) Women were taking off their clothes and writhing around on MTV.

For a long time, the dominant culture had been a representation of Christian values and ethics. It was wholesome. Fathers knew best and all that. But the culture slipped out of its grasp. It looked at the output of Hollywood, MTV, television, New York City media, the art world, and no longer saw itself represented. Christianity was deemed irrelevant, too boring and old-fashioned to attract a paying audience. The religious right confused—it still confuses—its cultural impotence with political impotence.

The year of the Summer of Mercy just happened to coincide with the first real emergence of the Westboro Baptist Church, centered in Topeka, Kansas. The church began its campaign in 1991 by claiming there was rampant homosexual activity in the city's parks, birthing both its God Hates Fags slogan and its bizarre selection of protest targets. Like the Summer of Mercy protesters, the Westboro Church was made up of outsiders. Fred Phelps, its patriarch, was from Mississippi, and his religious education had taken place in Tennessee and California. The church attracted few Kansas supporters; its membership was primarily made up of Phelps's own kin and assorted strays from around the country attracted by the possibility of yelling hateful things at grieving people.

If the Christian sensibility had been rendered invisible, they would force visibility. They would occupy space in the town center. They would go on television after every natural disaster and say it was god's punishment for gays and feminists. And if they could not sway the culture to return Christians to the position of moral arbiter, they would force the culture to conform to their ideals through legislative power. Suddenly there was political debate about whether people who were HIV-positive should be interned and quarantined. Suddenly abortion clinics were being asked to adhere to nonsensical regulations requiring a very specific width of hallways and to distribute confusing and medically inaccurate information about health care procedures. And suddenly my little church, whose sermons had mostly been about how to deal with doubt and disappointment, about neighborly love, about spiritually weathering god's capricious distribution of precipitation during harvest season, started hosting preachers who told us Muslims wanted to invade our homes and slit our throats in a holy war. Suddenly my Sunday school teacher was showing us pictures of mangled fetuses.

The rhetoric had an urgency. Abortion wasn't an ethical issue that could be intellectualized and debated. Abortion was the slaughter of the unborn. It was genocide, a second Holocaust. And people who were swayed by this eruption into the culture responded logically. If one believed there was a genocide going on, that abortion was murder and abortion doctors murderers, then violence seemed a justifiable response. Fuck conversation, fuck consciousness raising, there is murder going on in this place, and the address is in the fucking phone book.

There were those who preached peace and mercy. There were those who thought abortion was morally unacceptable, who went into the pulpits and public square and opinion pages of newspapers to make an ethical case for condemning abortion. They would pray the rosary silently outside of clinics. But no one remembers them today, not even in the anti-abortion movement. They remember Eric Rudolph, who bombed abortion clinics. They remember Shelley Shannon, Robert L. Dear Jr., Michael F. Griffin, and James Kopp, and all of the other religious militants.

Dr. George Tiller might have been Operation Rescue's specific target in part because Kansas was such a powerful symbolic background. It was America's heartland. It was a Christian stronghold, a conservative base of power. If they couldn't control Kansas, how could they even start to exert control over the rest of the nation?

But Tiller was an unmovable force. He was one of the few doctors willing to perform late-term abortions, and women came from all over the country to seek his care. For him, too, abortion was a moral issue, although in his moral universe women should have control over whether they became mothers, and their bodies should be considered as more than just incubators.

His obstinacy made him a visible target. When his clinic was firebombed, they cleaned up the mess and reopened immediately. A banner reading "Hell No We Won't Go" hung above the entrance. The callback to the Vietnam War protests was deliberate. He, like the original Catholic pro-life protesters, believed every life was sacred. A woman's life is sacred. His father, also a doctor, had provided abortions in secret when it was illegal, and Tiller saw the effects an illegal abortion could have on a woman's body, even if it did not kill her. He also saw the way mandatory motherhood had of trapping women in poverty, in abusive situations, and in addiction.

His clinic was bombed, he went back to work. His clinic was besieged by protesters for an entire summer, he went back to work. He received death threats, he went back to work. He was shot in both arms in a failed assassination attempt, he went back to work. And he went back to work with a flourish, in a red sports car he called Igor and a "go fuck yourself" attitude.

Then Scott Roeder followed him into church one Sunday morning and shot him in the head, killing him in front of his family, community, and church.

Like a lot of political men, Roeder was disappointing. He

could not hold down a job. His wife left him. He did not seem to have a coherent political or religious ideology. He became anti-government because he did not want to pay taxes. He did not oppose abortion because he believed in the sacred nature of all life. He did not seem very interested in the well-being of even his own estranged children.

There are those who believe abortion is as obvious an abomination as slavery was. That a life created must be guaranteed the possibility of flourishing. That all life must be protected and cherished, and that the ending of any life is not only a tragedy but a crime. It comes from the same place as the belief that holding a human life as property for your own purposes and profit is unacceptable. It is a system of evil that can be understood as such outside of conversations about gender and race, because it originates at a deeper level.

Then there are those who don't know what they believe. They were raised in religious families, they want to feel important, they are using the issue to hide their bias and frustrated impotence, they wanted to associate themselves with a particular demographic so they take on its beliefs as their own. Or they are simply looking for a justifiable, or maybe just an opportunistic, outlet for their dark murderous impulses.

One of the reasons these issues become intractable is that people have so little awareness as to the roots of their political beliefs. Unable to separate out politics from self-interest, unable to separate out a sense of self from political identity, they obfuscate and dodge and self-deceive. Tracing a political stance all the way to its source, whether that lies in religion or values or experience, is an act of self-interrogation few people are willing to undertake.

Some might say, disingenuously, that Tiller and Roeder were

engaged in essentially the same act. Tiller was destroying life through his abortion practice, and Roeder, through political assassination. The difference is in intention. Tiller intended to help create a world with less poverty and addiction, more autonomy for women, and fewer children raised in painful circumstances. This end was pursued not simply through abortion but through other kind acts, like inviting women to recuperate and gather strength in his and his wife's home. Agree or disagree with his methods, one can see a man living by his ideals, actively engaged in reshaping the world to reduce misery, and living by and through his well-considered principles.

We can grant no such grace to Roeder, who was only interested in destruction. Even if we can say that abortion is murder, it is still not right to go out and put an end to the murder through murderous violence. Not only because of the direct contradiction—condemning someone for committing murder and murdering them as punishment. Nor only because such violence does not accomplish much—maybe a few women were swayed not to go through with their scheduled procedures, but Tiller was replaced and the clinic stayed open. Tiller became a martyr, and a foundation was created in his name to provide funding for medical training, medical services to women in need, educational programs, and support for battling addiction and poverty.

If we are going to decide who is a hero, who is painted on the walls of government buildings, who is lionized, and who we should model our behavior after, we must consider the intention, the results, and the method. And I'm tired of thunder gods taking up all the public space.

Roeder became a hero to many in the anti-abortion cause. They raised money for his defense, they championed him on their forums. Meanwhile there are others who believe abortion is unacceptable and who, much like Tiller, have worked to create a better world. They built homes for pregnant women, allowing some who may have felt that bringing a child into their lives would be financially impossible, or irresponsible, to choose to continue the pregnancy. They advocated for social reform. They ministered and tried to instill hope. They counseled women and tried to move them out of destructive circumstances. Agree or disagree with their beliefs, one can see these people living by their ideals, actively engaged in reshaping the world to reduce misery, and living through their well-considered principles.

But for many followers of the anti-abortion cause, that is less interesting or dynamic or heroic than shooting someone in the face in a church in front of his children. Murder at least feels like doing something, even if in a lot of ways it is the opposite of doing something. In a world that resists change, that is soggy with sorrow and suffering, that washes out every little act of effort, pointing to a death and saying, "At least I did this," is much, much easier than the constant uncertainty that plagues those who go about their work of tending to others. "Is it enough, could I have done more?" Killing someone, dying young, martyrdom can also be cowardly acts.

Before Harper's Ferry, before John Brown became a martyr and was (falsely) credited with sparking the Civil War, which is credited with ending slavery, he was a murderer. He made his sons into murderers. He forced reluctant men to become murderers.

There was a lot of it going around. The raids into Kansas by proslavery forces from Missouri were leaving many dead, houses burned, towns terrorized. There was an attack on Lawrence; hundreds of vigilantes came across the border and more than a hundred people, including children, were left dead. The attack was revenge for attacks by antislavery forces, who had carried out raids on border towns against the proslavery families who lived there. Those attacks were . . . you get it.

Brown, who had been nearby but could not get his militia to Lawrence before the devastation was over, plotted a new round of revenge. He did not make it to the big, glorious fight of retribution, but he still was amped up. He would continue the fight, a decision made only on his own authority. Others who had been fighting a lot longer tried to dissuade him. He decided to attack proslavery families that had taken up residence in the state of Kansas. They had had nothing to do with the raids, but they supported the same cause. He, his sons, and the rest of the militia went from house to house, dragging out men and their sons in front of their terrified wives, and they executed them in the fields.

Many words have been spilled over the years, trying to decide whether these men were "innocent." There is no innocence in a corrupt system, some believe. The victims of this massacre were involved in proslavery organization, they supported turning Kansas into a slave state, and some had participated in intimidation at the polls to keep antislavery voters away. Anyone with a part in this system of oppression and death, in this argument, was culpable and should share in its punishment.

Others—who may or may not claim that the Civil War was about state's rights and may or may not defend displays of the Confederate flag because, after all, it's about history and heritage, not hate—would argue that the men and boys murdered by Brown's militia took no lives, did not participate in the raids, burned down no buildings, raped no women, and caused no terror, so ultimately they were innocent. And then the other side might say, well, they raped no women *that we know of*, and on and on.

We should all be able to agree that innocence does not truly exist. And that insistence on innocence as a metric of goodness only leads us to create other metrics that weigh certain behaviors in one group as harmless and the same behaviors in another group as proof of deviance. We have already decided what we believe about these people, innocent or not, and the math works backward from there.

But then "no such thing as innocence" is the language of the terrorist, whether the suicide bomber going into a market square or the supporter of drone warfare racking up undisclosed collateral damage.

All of our moral universes have these blank spaces of "well, but," the unknowable dark matter that looks like a void but maintains influence. We believe we are thinking in straight lines but instead get pulled in different directions by its impossible gravity without noticing we're off track.

If it's not about guilt or innocence, maybe it should just be about how no one deserves to bear the entire weight of the system in which they are caught. Complicity does not equal control. Participation does not imply full knowledge or an inability to change. Allowing an evil system to exist without protest or complaint is not worthy of death. Gaining privilege or material support from an evil system is not worthy of death. Being a prop to an evil system is not worthy of death.

All of these things are, however, worth accounting for. There should always be institutions that allow people to see both the evil of the system and their participation within it, and then they should be helped to take responsibility. That's not innocence and that's not guilt; that's wading in the murky waters in which we all swim and drink and piss. No one deserves to have one moment made emblematic of the entirety of their life, to have the future and the past rewritten by people who have nothing to do with them.

Nico put a podcast on the stereo as he cleaned the kitchen, and the more I listened the angrier I got. It was an investigation into a shooting. Baltimore police had shot and killed an armed eighteen-year-old who had fired his gun into the street.

I wasn't angry at the police. I was angry at the journalist. I was angry that she was interviewing this teenager's family, that I was hearing them insisting on his innocence and ultimate goodness. I was angry at Nico for putting the story on and asking me to listen. I was angry about being asked to care about this one specific person. With all of the violence and intimidation and indiscriminate death doled out by the police across this nation, why was I being asked to care about the death of someone who was participating in violence and endangering others?

The answer is, of course, because his life was taken from him. But I was so angry about being asked to care. He was shooting his gun at a car. There were many others around who he could have hurt. I imagined that if I were on the street and a man started shooting, I would want him to be removed as a threat as well.

But the anger, so consuming and quickly overwhelming, was surprising. Why anger and not disinterest? Why not just say, "You know what? I have such a backlog of podcast episodes and books and magazines and everything else, I don't really want to start something new?" I not only tried to justify my lack of interest, I started to attack the legitimacy of the project.

I didn't want to care, but my attempts at keeping myself from caring were not much different from the actions of those who dig into the backgrounds of unarmed people murdered by the police. Every time someone is shot down by the state, the media repeats the same useless debate. Was this person an angel or a devil? Everyone follows along, trying to suss out their innocence, pretending it's only logical to do so. Really, though, it is a cry from the masses: "Do I really have to care about this?" There are all sorts of contortions people will go through to avoid caring. I am no different.

If I care, where does that lead? Do I have to believe as well? Must I act? Will I have to reform and rethink? Must I claim solidarity with people I don't like? Will caring for this person mean I have to remove my care from someone else? What is the formula by which I can determine who is more worthy of care, and of how much care? Will I cry? Will I write a letter? Will I take to the streets? Will I have to? And if I do, will I ever be able to leave the streets, or will there always be a new reason, each time I refresh my social media feeds, to be out there, using my body and my unceasing wails to display my care, like a designated mourner, except no one is paying me for this shit and I might get kicked in the teeth by the cops for my efforts?

This is not an anecdote about an important lesson learned. After the anger and the argument, I did not revisit the case. I did not sit down and listen to the podcast and understand something new about my limited empathy and refusal of humanity. Mostly I just forgot about it.

It seemed like too much, but then all of it does. The children in overfull facilities on our border, those murdered by the police (armed or unarmed), the middle school girls trafficked on airplanes for the entertainment of billionaires, the bodies spat out by the Mediterranean Sea, the GoFundMe campaigns for things like rent and insulin, the overdoses in grocery stores and in front yards and at schools. All of it is too much. No wonder empathy is so selective. No wonder one starts fantasizing about a cleansing fire. No wonder the imagination stops at destruction, and can't conjure much on the other side of it. It's fucking exhausted.

It's not that I don't think the ends sometimes justify the means. I only wish every person on every side of every debate didn't think the same thing. I wish that every asshole didn't have the same definition of "means." I wish my religious education had not been so tightly intertwined with my political education, and I wish my political education had not been about all the things I should be against: homosexuality, abortion, premarital sex, gun control, mercy. I wish I had been instilled with an understanding of how to support something, rather than talk about it endlessly and ineffectively wring my hands as I watch things go wrong.

For a long time I was pro-choice in the sense of saying I was pro-choice and doing a quick search to see if the politician I was about to vote for also said they were pro-choice. It took me a while to understand that if I wanted reproductive freedom, that meant more than rhetoric or wearing a sassy Barbara Kruger T-shirt. It meant taking bodies from car to clinic door. It meant finding money when a pregnant person who needed an abortion couldn't. It meant politically organizing against legislation that dictated how wide a hallway in an abortion clinic had to be. It also meant listening to stories I didn't want to hear, of multiple abortions in a year, of sexual recklessness, of all the selfish behavior my ideological enemies accused my side of displaying and deciding to keep helping anyway. And now that the legality of abortion is entering another gray zone, it means filling your pants pockets with misoprostol and carrying it across borders. It means learning menstrual extraction techniques. It means disobeying, but not in a cool way—not a brick through the window or a punch to the face or a shout in the ear. It means disobeying laws that try to keep you from sustaining a person's life. It's not dramatic, it's not sexy, it's heavy lifting. Lives are heavy lifting.

I keep thinking about John Brown's sons. I think about the son who was hanged, the son who killed himself, and the son who refused direct orders to help in the massacre. They all believed in the righteous cause of abolition. Their lives revolved around it in one way or another, either getting them killed or by forcing them to survive the execution of their own father. But what it meant to them, outside of these acts of violence, remains mostly a mystery.

Terrorists, radicals, revolutionaries are all meant to die young. Surviving the moment of potential martyrdom is in its own way a kind of tragedy. You give your life to the cause, whether or not you die for it. And often living for it, so rarely factored into the possible methods of devotion, is the heavier burden.

There are interviews with former members of the Provisional IRA, part of an oral history project conducted by an American university, which offered protections to allay the subjects' fears of prosecution or being held accountable for their actions and so encourage unfiltered conversation. It wasn't the acts of violence they recounted that shocked me. It was their disappointment.

The Catholics of Northern Ireland faced constant discrimination when it came to employment, housing, schooling, and other basic human rights. What radicalized many and led them to join paramilitary groups, though, wasn't the discrimination but the violence. Peaceful protests were met with bricks and fists. Later they'd be met with bullets and bombs. Some were enticed to join to provide protection for their community, only to find themselves sliding easily from defensive to offensive violence. Then, soon, strategically targeted assassination turned into occasional indiscriminate violence and murder.

It was for a cause, for a better world. They were fighting for a united Ireland. They were fighting for a socialist state. They got neither. When the Good Friday Agreement ended the war, there was to be no union, and the boom and bust that was coming would prove there was to be nothing but rapacious capitalism.

Many of the interviews were with people who were exhausted, demoralized, and angry. Asked to commit atrocities for the possibility of a better future, only to have that future never materialize, they dissolved themselves in drink and resentment. They weren't able to die for their cause, but they were asked to kill for it. And not just to kill the occupying British force. They killed kids. They killed mothers and fathers. They killed whoever happened to be around when the bomb went off.

Maybe those deaths would have been bearable if the ends had been attained. If today there were a socialist, united Ireland, a land free from discrimination offering a life of dignity for all, if Britain had been forced to admit its colonialist horrors and the crimes against humanity committed during the occupation, maybe the ghosts created by these acts of violence would stay quiet. Maybe they could find rest as martyrs for a cause. Maybe even in death they could understand that they'd played a role in the creation of a new world, that their lives had to end so that others could begin.

Instead, they haunt. Not given the dignity of a choice, dragged into situations that were not their own, their deaths, and their lives, were stripped of meaning. No longer a mother, a son, a lover, a poet, a post office worker, a good friend, a maker of splendid lemon cakes, now they were just victims. Their names live on, but only in the cold marble of memorials.

And for the terrorists, where there once was certainty, now there was doubt. The act of killing no longer had its original meaning, and those deaths could no longer be disregarded as a terrible necessity. The ends didn't come, so they were stuck with the means, and not all could bear it. Many were furious at a government that sold them out, that denied their legitimate cause, and at all of the men who directed the violence but did not wage it.

When I wonder about John Brown's sons, I wonder about their late nights. Their cause was just, and their side won, and I wonder if that wiped it clean for them. So many lives were lost in the years to come, maybe it was hard to take stock of which were ended by you and which by a soldier, which by the state. All the blood became one big pool, the sources indiscriminate. And you, you are just another member of a movement, not a single individual with free will. Perhaps if your side wins, you can think of yourself as an instrument of fate, rather than as a person who will have to account for your actions. There are certainly those on the other side in Northern Ireland, members of loyalist paramilitaries or British soldiers, who sleep fine.

So much of the rhetoric around soldiers' trauma is about dealing with what they saw or what happened to them, rather than reconciling what they did. We cannot for a moment welcome doubt. Not for the sake of the soldier who took a life, nor for the men who ordered them to do it. The cause is always just, the death always necessary. If the people in power had to admit doubt about their orders, it wouldn't just be the dead soldiers haunting them, but all the ghosts of all the people killed by all the soldiers they commanded, like some morbid, inescapable pyramid scheme.

John Brown got to be a martyr. He didn't have to live with what he had done. Some of the leaders of the Provisional IRA kept their hands clean. They entered into political life, denying all involvement in the violence.

The situation for Catholics has improved. One can't say which burden was carried forward by which individual soul, but it's those who died in glory who are painted up on the murals. The priests, the nuns, the mothers, the aid workers, the doctors, the politicians, the advocates, the musicians, the artists, the teachers—anybody who willingly took a load upon their backs—show up a lot less.

I was at a bar with an attorney. It's in Chicago, and it's the last holdout in the neighborhood for day drinkers and lowlifes who just want to drink bad whiskey while listening to Pantera while sitting on a plastic patio chair in a neighborhood that is mostly gyms and shops selling fifty-dollar T-shirts with ironic slogans. Once you get through the women in athleisure-wear pushing baby strollers to optimize their footstep count for the day, it's a cool refuge from a world that demands constant assessment and improvement. You can be your true scumbag self here. Also, there's free popcorn.

He's an activist, a legal saboteur, taking on hard political cases and pro bono work and the limited financial and social prosperity that comes with it. He's brown, his family is brown, and he's been telling me about recent Tinder dates with white girls who want him to role-play the maniacal fundamentalist terrorist and the scared, innocent hostage with them in bed.

"So do you?"

He shrugs.

We've been talking about the recent demonstrations—who can even keep track of which one it was back then? The protests against police murdering someone? The protests against Trump's inauguration? The protests against a white nationalist gathering? The protests against abortion bans? The protests against police murdering someone else? There is always something new to be against.

But the organizers of this particular demonstration, who my friend knew and worked with, were frustrated by some of the new members. After years of hard work, of activism and organization, there were suddenly large numbers of people on the street, and the violent idiots had started to show up. They didn't seem to believe in the cause. They skipped the organizational meetings and had only a passing knowledge of the ideology that created the movement. They just wanted to put a trash can through a window. Or throw a brick at a cop. Or "punch a Nazi." They escalated things because they were bored, and often invited a violent response from the police and counter-protesters. And then they disappeared until the next rally.

Which is not to say that Nazis don't need to be punched, or that Chase Bank doesn't deserve a trashcan through its window. But that when there's violence, there should be a strategy. There should be a conversation about legitimate targets and execution, so that vulnerable people can be protected from the consequences. These guys, who probably watched *Fight Club* and decided they wanted to start their own fight club, were only interested in the fight for the means, not for the ends. They had a way of taking the story away from the organizers.

My friend, though, was defending the chaos bringers. "I think leftist movements need to stop being scared of violence. A little indiscriminate bloodshed can be good for a movement. No revolution ever happened without it."

"The minute you kill a child, you lose all moral high ground," was the only thing I could think of to say. We squabbled the rest of the night, him talking about the gains made by the Provisional IRA during its struggle, me pointing to people like Bernadette Devlin and Edward Daly. He spoke of atrocities committed by the other side, I talked about how once violence became normalized a socialist movement got taken over by murderers, and those murderers betrayed the socialist origins. There was no bridging the gap between us.

Am I just too hopelessly bourgeois? I assume that is what he thinks of me. Maybe I am too satisfied with the status quo and not truly supportive of real change, not what it could bring and not what it costs.

It's possible. It's also possible I am tired of having someone explain to me why this person deserves to die and this person deserves to live. I am tired of people who think they know the ideal organization of the world.

(I am an exit)

That's what the government does isn't it it sings to you without you knowing it and every morning you have a song in your head and you don't know you don't know how it got in there it just sounds like your own voice.

JOHANNA HEDVA

People, who still have a spark of humanity! Pull yourselves together! Hear my cry! A simple old man's cry, a cry of a son of a nation that beloved its own freedom as well as freedom of others above all, above its own life! Pull yourselves together! It's not too late yet!

RYSZARD SIWIEC

DRIVING INTO JUNCTION CITY from the east is almost exactly the same now as it was twenty years ago. The same fort and military structures on the right, the same tanks on the hill with children climbing over them on the left. It's the same truck stops and the same fast-food restaurants, the same massive cups to be filled with soda or iced tea, although now there's a selection of gourmet coffees as well as the urn of muddy, ash-tasting slosh that has been baking in that carafe for who knows how long.

The main difference is on the radio. There used to be a great rock station within range here that played the angry wailing of young white men and a handful of angry white women. Nirvana, Pearl Jam, Nine Inch Nails, Smashing Pumpkins. I would wait until we made the curve around the hill, when the city came into sight, to tune into it on my Walkman. Before then, it would only be static, the occasional chord or squeal piercing through.

Now, though, that station is gone. Or the programming has changed to what is popular now, which is relentless cheer. Tiny pop singers bouncing up and down and telling me I can do it, whatever *it* is. Reach for those goals, achieve those dreams, I am a tiger, I am a fighter, I am a warrior. "You don't know me," I think grumpily.

If we had turned south at this point, we would reach Herington in thirty minutes or so. It would be indistinguishable from any of the other small towns on this particular drive. Most of my extended family lived in Topeka, and we made this drive every two weeks or so in our silvery blue minivan. Two and a half hours to get from the midpoint of Kansas to the fairly far east of Kansas. A stop in Junction City for gas, fast food, and potty breaks, as my mother called them, even after we stopped being children.

Before Junction City and after, there'd be small towns off the highway, with yards that ran right up to the street, no curbs or sidewalks to mark the transition. Straggly trees, big houses not recently painted, haze from the burning fields surrounding the town as the farmers transitioned between seasons. Small towns with main streets just a few blocks long, some with thriving storefronts and some with FOR LEASE signs. A lot of the life here revolved around farming and the fort, so you'd see a lot of camouflage, a lot of pickup trucks, a lot of men with sunburns on the back of their necks and their arms from wrist to mid-bicep.

It's a strange mismatch now to listen to the empowering

auto-tuned chirpings of pop stars telling me how great I'm going to do against this backdrop. Not that there aren't some signs of new life. All over rural Kansas, there's an effort to stop the population drain to the cities. To convince the younger folk that these small towns that to teenagers seem like something to endure, something to be ashamed of, something to escape, aren't so bad after all. There are new restaurants, farm-to-table instead of a new franchise. Salina has a microbrewery. Assaria has a Northern Italian restaurant with a decent wine list, built in the old high school that got shut down. The golden beet soup is excellent.

But the fort still looms large, because for some it's still the only chance for a different kind of life. The service is noble, yes, it's part of family tradition, yes, but for some it's also the only option to see the world, go to college, make enough money to buy a house. Whether you are going or staying.

That's what the army promises. We'll make a man out of you, no matter what gender you might be. The discipline, the grit, the obedience you learn will propel you into the future. A better future. Not the narrative that flows naturally from your beginnings, a story recreating the conditions in which you were raised. Broken-down cars on the front lawn. A smack across the face, a belt across your back. The humiliation and physical violence of high school. The constant rejection from the desired object. Going to the fort will disrupt that story, allow you to start over with a more charismatic protagonist, a better plot, more comfortable settings. Or so we're told.

More than twenty years later, it's all pretty much the same. There's nothing to commemorate that this is where the Oklahoma City bombing was plotted. There's no marker near the fort to acknowledge that it created those "new men." Because it did rewrite the stories of at least those few white men. It took their past and gave them a future as domestic terrorists.

Being asked to murder strangers radicalized Timothy McVeigh. As he himself said, going to war in the Persian Gulf, being ordered to murder Iraqi soldiers, including soldiers who were in the act of surrendering, and realizing the reasons given to justify the war—protection of Kuwait, reining in a tyrant, establishing peace in a troubled region—were bullshit, this is when he started to turn. He knew he was being asked to kill people to protect economic and corporate interests, and it gnawed at him. Being lied to by his government gnawed at him.

His biography before that, well, it's indistinguishable from most of the town boys I went to school with. Not the farm kids, who had responsibilities and a role to play within a family and a tradition that was passed down to them. No, the ones with absent parents who worked late as waitresses and factory workers and at the quarry. The ones whose families were talked about in low tones at the grocery store. The ones who had to take after-school jobs at the grocery store to help provide for the family. The ones with single moms, the ones who had different colored lunch cards than the rest of us, the ones who didn't speak up in class or take days off during senior year to tour college campuses. There was one who came to school wearing a Hitler mustache on Hero's Day during homecoming week. It was a joke. There were several who compulsively drew pictures of guns in their notebooks during algebra. My neighbors, my classmates, my friends.

They did well in the military. They found direction there, someone who would tell them what to do. It gave them purpose. They got to use the guns they had before only dreamed about. All of that anger and resentment and propensity for violence was finally given a direction and a channel. Go shoot some Iraqis. Yes, sir.

But this wasn't a righteous war. The enemy wasn't Nazis or Commies or any other obvious doers of evil. They were just guys. And the cause wasn't noble. It wasn't to stop Hitler from taking over the world, it was a bunch of poor kids from small towns sent off to risk death to protect corporate interests. It was CIA shit. It was profiteering shit. It was empire-building shit. A lot of guys came back traumatized, disillusioned, and looking for someone to explain the world to them in a way that did not sound like a lie. And who they found, ready to embrace them, were white nationalists.

It's reported that white nationalist groups and militias peak in membership during and right after wartime, as the vets coming home, with their PTSD and their us-against-them mentality and their newly acquired proficiency with weaponry, search for a new enemy. It's not at all worrying, then, that we are locked into an endless war on several different fronts.

There isn't any counterculture anymore. There isn't really even any good drug culture now that marijuana is legal and has become just another part of money culture. Punk bands sell their songs for commercials, artists hang out with billionaire collectors, writers have become bourgeois. There are no bohemians, no voluntary marginalization, no outsiders. Everyone has bought in, everyone wants to get paid.

The point of counterculture wasn't whether or not it "worked." It didn't matter if hippie communes were intolerable, if living-off-the-land movements tended to break apart come winter, if free love was mostly used by men to avoid any kind of emotional responsibility to the people they were putting their dicks into. It didn't matter if the antiwar movements ultimately failed, if alternative schools lasted only a couple years, if squats eventually were turned into "artistic" lofts and sold to bankers. What mattered was the attempt.

The counterculture works through influence, not dominance. Ideas wander in and out. Some are rejected, others co-opted. Most of it looks ridiculous from a distance. When something does happen to be good, outsiders swarm in, say they're the inventors, and make a profit from it. It's unlikely that the person who originates a really good idea ever sees any benefit from that. And while that is unfortunate, again: that is not the point.

The point of the counterculture is that it gives you a safe place to land once you have that moment of awakening, once you realize that our society is sick. The government is trying to kill you, corporate culture poisons everything, we are distracted from the spiritual emptiness of our lives by shopping, pornography, and social media. Once you have that realization, you'll look around for alternatives. Something new to do, rather than just something new to think.

The political left in America has abandoned this form of experimentation and collectivity. Not that small-town white guys with rage issues and military service were ever wholeheartedly welcomed in Bohemia. But now, the left criticizes culture rather than builds it. They theorize, they speculate, they cynically roll their eyes, but they don't engage. They go to grad school, they intellectualize. They set impossible rules and standards, creating exclusionary spaces maintained through shunning techniques when all the unwritten rules are not followed. All experimentation is done through the self, through the body and identity rather than through social engagement. You are left alone in your pursuit of something new and real, and in the end you are left even more isolated than you had been previously.

The right, though. They understand the primal need each

individual has for recognition. Every person in this world needs to feel they play a part in the world. But as family structures break down, communities break down, neighborhoods break down, employment breaks down, all of these places we have turned to and sought recognition from can no longer provide it. So we find ourselves looking to society at large to grant what used to be much more localized.

Every person needs to be seen, heard, and understood as something more complex than just their identity markers. You are not your race, your gender, your generation, your sexuality, your class, your religion. Or at least you are not only any of these things. You are more complicated and more sophisticated than all of that, but the larger world stereotypes and simplifies. The new world of identity politics and social media erases all of that context more violently than ever before. Everyone you come in contact with, because they don't know your family, your friends, your schools, your character, your astrological markers, or anything else about you, gets to decide who you are and what your story is, based on a tweet or a picture of your face.

The right takes that need for recognition and amps it up. You are not only seen, you are superior. You get to step into a world created wholly for you. There is an instant community, an instant set of new beliefs, an instant story of how the world works that makes sense to you. White nationalists are extremely good at showing up for one another and providing support. Their story explains why the government is trying to kill them (because it's run by Jews), why society is sick (because we've strayed from the Judeo-Christian tradition of Western civilization), and they offer an alternative to the empty consumerist culture that they blame liberals for creating. They will help get you off drugs, they will introduce you to your new gender-conforming girlfriend, they will help you get on your feet financially.

For a very long time, a small segment of our population avoided self-knowledge by asserting dominance. They projected anything they didn't want to be onto another identity. They wanted to be rational, so they called women overly emotional, histrionic, hysterical. They wanted to be civilized, so they called black people savages. They wanted to be refined, so they called poor people brutes. They wanted to be manly, so they called the French effeminate. And so on. Stereotyping other people isn't just a way of cataloging other people, it's a way of cataloging ourselves.

The dominant segment kept this system in place by basically refusing to allow anyone else to insist on their own reality. Women were kept silent, racial minorities were kept silent, religious minorities were kept silent, the poor were kept quiet, and Americans pretended they couldn't understand French. Now, of course, that silence has been broken, and if you want to know how a woman is, how a black person is, you can pretty quickly figure that out. You can ask. You can read one of their books. You can listen to a TED talk. With almost zero effort, you can discover rather than assume.

But that requires action on your end as well. If you want to be seen as rational, you have to start to be rational, consistently. If you want to be seen as civilized, you have to practice civility. You have to make yourself intelligent. You have to figure out how to dress yourself. You have to invest some time and effort in presenting these qualities in a way that can be recognized by others. You also have to figure out what your qualities actually are, whether they are strengths or weaknesses or both. You have to consider that maybe being emotional, brutal, and effeminate aren't the worst things in the world. Maybe there are inner resources you had no idea you had, things that can be embraced and utilized, things kept stifled and shamed for so very long, and you'll have to deal with the regret that you avoided this self-knowledge for so long.

It's the process of individuation, and it's exhausting. If you look around at our culture, you can see immediately that no one wants to do this work. How much easier to rely on association and identity. How much easier to assume there's something external that makes you special and interesting rather than something internal. Or if it is internal, how much easier if it's something you are born with rather than something you cultivate.

Society at large is not up to the task of recognition, so why would anyone pursue this goal of individuation? Contemporary society is selective in what it recognizes, things like status, power, and achievement. There are other ways of being recognized. We will acknowledge pain, trauma, and vulnerability. At least it's a form of recognition. But some traumas are deemed more important, more traumatizing, than others. So either way, you are stuck in a competition for attention.

People who aren't up for the competition, they end up alienated. And without the internal organization of individuation to steady them, they're open to persuasion. Without their selves being seen, without their pains being acknowledged, they find it hard to see others as whole beings or to acknowledge others' pain. So they find white nationalism.

I mean, some of them. Some people are fucking evil, let's not forget that.

First there was Ruby Ridge. A man who believes in the coming apocalypse, which will include a violent showdown with a tyrannical federal government, is entrapped in a weapons charge because the cops hope that will force him to inform on the white nationalist group to which he has loose ties. But he won't agree to snitch and also won't show up for his court date. The federal government invades his property, murders his young son, kills his dog, and blows his wife's head off in front of her surviving children while she has a baby in her arms. The government taunts him over a loudspeaker, asking him to send out his wife after they have already murdered her.

There was an attempted cover-up, which mostly failed, but those responsible for the murder of a child and a woman and a dog and the terrorizing of a man and his children are not held accountable. No one even loses their job.

All of it could have been avoided if a racist judicial system had not let the white nationalist movement get out of control unmonitored in the first place, if people in law enforcement decided to treat the people they came in contact with as human beings, or if people with power ever thought the best thing to do might be to retreat, to let things slide, or to de-escalate, rather than forcing things to the inevitable conclusion of bloodshed and horror.

In the midst of the standoff at Ruby Ridge, in Idaho, people gathered to protest. They were mostly white nationalists. It's not clear if it was only white nationalists who cared or if the white nationalists scared off any reasonable protesters, but that is who was there. The association was unfortunate, making it look like the government was taking a strong hand against neo-Nazis, rather than terrorizing a family after a year of harassment. Timothy McVeigh was paying attention.

Then there was Waco. A man who believes in the coming apocalypse, which will include a violent showdown with a tyrannical federal government, is forced into a standoff with government forces. The government comes up with a reason having to do guns to cause a confrontation, despite putting a great number of children at risk. They refuse to listen to people who understand the people living in the compound, believing their own psychological profiles will be enough.

The government keeps escalating the situation, shining bright lights into the windows of the compound, playing noise and loud music at deafening levels all night long to denying anyone inside sleep or peace. They cut access to power and water. They tell the gathered media that the people inside are crazy, are pedophiles, are monsters capable of almost anything.

The government almost certainly fired first. They killed the compound's dogs, they rolled tanks into the structure. The sniper who shot a woman in the head as she was holding her baby at Ruby Ridge was there on active duty. The burning of the compound and the deaths of dozens of people was broadcast on live television. The government created lies to justify its decisions: there was pedophilia going on within the compound, there was rampant child abuse, babies were being beaten.

A crowd gathered. There were white supremacists, gun rights activists, McVeigh, and then a lot of curious folks who wanted to see the madman burn. When he did, along with most of his followers and wives and children, the media was content to keep the government's story going. David Koresh was a child-fucking monster, everyone there chose to die, the outcome was inevitable. INSIDE THE COMPOUND headlines sold tabloids and respectable newspapers alike for weeks.

The counternarrative, then, mostly circulated among people who identified with those murdered at Ruby Ridge and Waco: the religious, gun owners, white nationalists. They weren't wrong about one thing: the government absolutely does not care about you. The dehumanization at both locations wasn't the method, it was the objective. Turn these people into monsters, remove their dignity, aim guns at their children, lie about them to the press and to other law enforcement. Not only that, but actively ignore the people who know the human beings you are targeting, refuse to see them as people with names, histories, problems, complications, emotions, hobbies, interests, bad habits, families.

Of course, this isn't new information. Yet somehow every group that becomes a government target is surprised to find this out. They haven't listened to the groups that have long known. They don't listen to the people who don't look like them, who have been dealing with beatings and executions by the police for decades. They don't listen to the women who are raped by police, they don't listen to the homeless who are pissed on, burned, beaten, laughed at. They don't listen to the Iraqis stripped naked and tortured and sexually assaulted by their female US military guards.

They certainly didn't listen when, more than a decade before Waco, a black liberation group called MOVE, holed up in a Philadelphia building, was besieged and firebombed by the police force. There, too, the government used the well-being of women and children as the excuse for executing a bunch of women and children. Eleven people died, including five kids. No one in the government or the police, no one who planned or participated in the raid, suffered any consequences, although one MOVE member, a woman who survived, was immediately sent to jail.

Listening is difficult. When someone comes to you with "I have a problem," your brain so often wants to shout in response, "But what about mine?" When a bunch of people come at you with "I have a problem," that "what about mine what about mine what about mine" can become an earworm. McVeigh was Mr. Whataboutmine. When he saw a fellow soldier wearing a T-shirt that read Black Power, he went out and bought one that said White Power. He seemed to feel the pain of being lied to by his government more acutely than he felt the pain of the Iraqis losing their lives as a result. Seeing himself as a few unchangeable things—white and American—made it impossible to expand the empathy he sincerely seemed to feel for similar people who lost their lives in their struggle against the United States government to anyone in the same fight who didn't share his markers. Trapped in his own identity politics, he couldn't gain the perspective to see that their situations were shared.

Some people use their "what about mine" to inflict the same problems on others. Some use their time spent in camps to justify putting other people in camps. Some use their time being beaten with a belt to justify beating others with a belt. When will someone pay attention to my pain, they cry as they stomp their boot onto the head of another, as they press their knee onto the neck of another.

Listening is hard, in part because listening, and speaking, is never enough. The documentation of trauma will never be enough to make traumatizing policies stop. And we're tragically bad at figuring out the true source of pain. We point to the administrator rather than the authority, we take systemic issues personally, we look for scapegoats and easy fixes. We assume the reasons for and the authority ordering the murder of black citizens and white nationalists to be very different, rather than part of the same process.

Terry Nichols, McVeigh's coconspirator, bought a house in Herington, Kansas. It was close to Fort Riley, where he and McVeigh had been stationed, and it seemed as good a place as any to build a bomb.

Like John Brown, McVeigh did not believe in innocence. McVeigh decided the government had turned tyrannical, and one must act under such circumstances. The building he and Nichols targeted was symbolically and tactically important. It housed an office of the Bureau of Alcohol, Tobacco, and Firearms, the agency that shared responsibility with the FBI for the sieges at Ruby Ridge and Waco. It housed recruiting offices for the marines and the army, which sent men to die and murder in foreign nations to support corporate interests. It housed an office of the Drug Enforcement Agency, which sent so many kids and poor people into the prison industrial complex. (Especially black and brown people, although it's unlikely any of the conspirators, who had bonded in part over their unwillingness to work with black colleagues in the army, thought or cared much about that.) The people who worked in those offices didn't matter. The association was enough to justify their deaths.

The children at the daycare center who died were merely collateral damage. Killing children, killing civilians, had long been considered just part of the struggle. The ends, the means, all that.

McVeigh didn't even try that hard not to get caught. He seemed to enjoy his status as political martyr, and the fact that the state decided to murder him wasn't exactly a surprise. He calmly explained his reasoning to almost any interviewer who would ask, and I became fascinated with reading and watching these conversations. Because his logic is the same as that of any individual fighting for freedom under oppression. It is the same language as that of Ryszard Siwiec, who set himself on fire in Warsaw in 1968, of Ulrike Meinhof, who quit her job as a journalist to become a terrorist in 1970s Germany, of Palestinian freedom fighters, Northern Irish paramilitary members, young radical teenagers under the sway of a fanatic. It may seem disingenuous to conflate all these disparate figures, but their rhetoric—of freedom, of awakenings, of justice, of necessity—is almost always the same. There is a barrier between us and freedom, and this barrier must be met with force.

Timothy McVeigh had a message. Violence is a form of communication. I reject the medium in the same way I reject all who decide death and chaos are somehow a magical portal to a fairer, better world.

Emma Goldman and Alexander Berkman were having an argument. He was in jail for his assassination attempt against industrialist Henry Clay Frick. She was out of jail for now, always being harassed by the police for distributing information about birth control or losing control of the crowd at one of her speeches, something like that. They had been lovers, they remained close friends.

President McKinley had just been assassinated. Goldman happened to be familiar with the kid who did it, a young man named Leon Czolgosz, who claimed an anarchist cause. Czolgosz was a troubled young working-class man, who had been radicalized by a speech made by Goldman. He hung around the anarchist groups, but the leaders of those groups reported that he did not engage much in the discussion. He had problems as a poor man in nineteenth-century America, and the anarchists told him who the enemy was: the rich, the industrialists, the president. He alone decided to commit this violent act.

Goldman praised Czolgosz. He had not killed the president for his own good but as an ideal act, for the good of all people. McKinley was an enemy of the steel workers, of men who toiled at slaughterhouses and women who sweated at textile factories, of the anarchists, and of the labor movement. It's not clear how much Czolgosz thought about all of this, but Goldman was quick to claim him as an ally. He must have done it because of the inhumane annexation of the Philippines! He must have done it because of the president's close ties to Wall Street! It escaped her, the possibility that it was simply because he was a fucked-up guy with violent, antisocial tendencies who listened to some speeches that told him there were a couple people who were to blame for the way his life had gone, so he picked one of them and shot him in the stomach. It was useful for her to assume he was a thoughtful, rational actor in the political drama, rather than what he was, which was a dreamer, a romantic who felt the degradation of labor more keenly than most and who longed for a better world.

The argument, then, was over whether the assassination of McKinley had any chance of creating that better world, a world where bodies are not broken in factories, slaughterhouses, and mills, where the poor are given time for leisure and the pursuit of beauty, where bosses and police and politicians are there not to exploit the populace but to protect and nurture it. Berkman said no. A would-be assassin himself, he rejected the notion that the killing of a president did anything to help usher in this new world.

He wrote to Goldman from prison, "Indeed, it is at once the greatest tragedy of martyrdom and the most terrible indictment of society that it forces the noblest men and women to shed human blood, though their souls shrink from it. The more imperative it is that drastic methods of this character be resorted to only as a last extremity. To prove of value they must be motivated by social rather than individual necessity and be aimed against a direct and immediate enemy of the people."

McKinley did not count. Nor, truly, does any president. Simply a manifestation of a country's will, a president in dying leaves a vacuum for but a moment. More of the same is quick to rush in and fill the void. Killing leaders leaves behind what they had been leading, from followers to enablers to infrastructure. Unless your plan is to wipe out half the world, there is no uprooting whatever evil is personified in a president or a dictator or a prime minister with one simple shot. It can instead make the evil harder to control, which the anarchists discovered as they were rounded up in mass arrests, tortured, and unjustly imprisoned after the death of McKinley.

Violence can be a tool of the oppressed, but only if it is surgical. To take a life does too much to the human spirit, if humanity remains within the killer. Berkman's own assassination attempt had been against a man who was poised to cause violence and death to steel-mill workers, having called in the Pinkertons to break their strike. Nine workers died the first day of fighting. Another industrialist was unlikely to make the same call or cause the same bloodshed, making Frick's murder strategic and, in the logic of the anarchists, justified.

Goldman was outraged at Berkman's letter, not understanding the power the lone wolf would gain over American society before too long. The white guy ill-equipped to deal with modern society and its harsh edges, listening to riled-up speeches about how this person is to blame for our situation, this group is ruining things for all of us. With easy access to weapons of mass death, he could walk into a crowded room and try to create a new world out of blood. Or just get on the news.

We are living in a world of Timothy McVeigh's creation, where every man gets to decide for himself what reality is, and where so many young men decide their only possible contribution to the world is their list of grievances. They lack the imagination or the emotional intelligence to see that their struggles are shared across the world, or to see that they have selves behind their whiteness, beyond their American birth certificate.

McVeigh said that he had considered assassinating Janet Reno, the woman who gave the orders for the siege at Waco. But McVeigh was no Berkman. He was thoughtful but not intellectual. He read unquestioningly the most heinous racist garbage that circulates among those curious about white nationalism. He was an arrogant loner, not part of a larger movement. He enjoyed violence and the thrills of carnage, but he did not understand the psychic toll it took on everyone involved. He came from the John Brown tradition. He wanted terror, and he wanted bodies.

(Reno reportedly gave the order to engage at Waco after subordinates lied to her that there were children being sexually and physically abused. This was also her justification for pursuing fabricated Satanic Panic cases alleging ritualistic sexual abuse during her time as a prosecutor. The evils done, the suffering caused, the blood spilled in the name of protecting imaginary vulnerable children will never cease.)

Like copies of a copy, the white men causing mass death, fantasizing about being the next Timothy McVeigh, are all blurry and sad replications. They only want to recreate the destructive swagger, not the intent. They don't even need real atrocities to radicalize them—they are all freaked out about the coming white genocide, the supposed unfair distribution of romantic and sexual attention from femoids to males, the threat posed to Western civilization by postmodernism.

Unable to grapple with their—with all of our—cosmic insignificance, and incapable of the curiosity required to look for answers in philosophy or politics or art, they project their inability to thrive onto the world. They lack the imagination to picture a world that would allow them to be at peace within it. They only want to destroy this one for not immediately accepting them. And they are too cowardly to reject the world by merely killing themselves; they have to have company when they go.

We create these men. From a school system that creates good little workers and not humans with a rich internal world, to a competition-based romantic life, to a medical system that tells us any inability to function in a sick world is pathology and that behavior must be contained via medication and a diagnosis, to . . . to . . . to . . . I am boring myself just typing this out. And the resignation and acceptance that chokes any possibility of change, that is going to get us all killed.

I watched a movie about a bright young woman who saved the world by destroying an entire city's worth of people. I watched a movie about an alienated young man who was so beaten down by society he decided to dress up in a costume and become a super villain, sowing chaos. I watched a movie about a caring white mother whose neighborhood is overrun by dark-faced threats and who decides to eradicate them all herself with a gun. I watch movie after movie where men and women decide they are the only ones who can save the world, wearing either a cop's badge or a cape. I watched a movie with a man so overcome with grief he decides to destroy an entire city. Another man, wearing a mask, stops him by killing him.

Saving the world, destroying the world, what is the difference at this point?

I watch a lot of old news reports about Timothy McVeigh online, and I sneer a little at the feigned incredulity of the commentators who talked about it. "Who could do something like this?" "What could ever motivate such an act?" Well, we all watched seventy-six people burn to death on live television in a situation created by our own government, could that possibly be it? The only thing I'm incredulous about is the lack of a mass, organized response by the people of this country to demand accountability and consequences for the death of those citizens. I can't help but think if there had been one maybe it would have stopped McVeigh from thinking in his poor, dumb, white-nationalist-propagandized brain that a good way to respond to mass death is to create some more. When I watch his *60 Minutes* interview, I don't see a dead-eyed monster. I see the guys I grew up with, the ones I was a little afraid of but went to the creek with anyway.

There were two mass shootings this week. One by a man who left behind a manifesto saying he had to stop the Mexicans coming into our country and overpowering the white race. The other by a man who started off by killing his sister.

The leftists are arming themselves. They're joking about guillotines and Bolsheviks, bragging about punching Nazis. They are unironically posting pictures of a young Stalin and crushing on him. They are dreaming of revolution so they don't have to live in the society as it exists. They seem to think the world would be much easier to rebuild if it is first turned to ash.

Centrists keep comparing every woman politician to some character in *Harry Potter*, that is, after they announce proudly their own status as a Hufflepuff or a Ravenclaw. Those are the only books they seem to have read, the story of a young man who is born special, who must go to war against the forces of darkness.

People on the right post videos about the QAnon conspiracy, a belief that a circle of powerful conspirators from Hollywood and the Democratic Party run a child-sex-trafficking ring, which has inspired believers to run off with guns in the name of rescuing the endangered, imaginary children.

It's all the same story, at once so boring and so terrifying.

I want to blow up a building. I want to join the Red Army Faction. I want to drag my enemies out of their houses at night and slay them with bayonets. I want to hole up in a compound with like-minded people and shut out the world and stockpile guns. I want to rid the world of evil and create change by destroying it first. But I'm not dumb enough to think any of that would help anything.

Because I see the tyranny of my own nation, a nation that facilitates genocide because we don't want to upset our oil allies. A nation that allows a militarized police to murder with impunity unarmed men and women because they are black, because they are mentally ill, because they moved their arm a bit, because they might be undocumented, because they were going to testify, because they were a whistleblower, because they had a phone in their hand. A nation that dehumanizes its citizenry and its guests at the border as a matter of policy, a nation that destabilizes the world for its own interests and then rejects the asylum claims of its inhabitants. A nation that decides for other nations who should lead them, how they should spend their money, with whom they should go to war. A nation that executes innocent men. A nation that executes anybody. A nation that allows pharmaceutical companies to set prices so high people are dying as they try to ration their insulin. A nation that imprisons so many black men, so many poor men, and then uses their forced labor for its economic gain. A nation that allows corporations to profit off the imprisonment of others, that allows those corporate prisons to deny medical care, psychiatric care, educational services, the touch of a loved one on a visit. A nation that floods the world with propaganda about how great we are, how strong, what amazing freedoms we promise, and then sends the people who believe it back to their deaths when they show up here. A nation that can't figure out how to educate its populace, how to feed its populace, how to house its populace, how to keep its populace healthy. A nation that can't figure out how to try its war criminals for war crimes. A nation that justifies torture with legal language. A nation that wants to suck the last drop of fossil fuels out of the earth and use it to power a chemical plant that is dumping poison into a river and giving children leukemia. A nation that wouldn't recognize the god it claims to worship if it ran into him at the bar.

I was fourteen when I watched seventy-six people burn to death on live television. I was sixteen when, exactly two years later, my teacher switched on the news so we could all watch the aftermath of a truck filled with fertilizer and explosives parked in front of a government building. And even at that age, as dumb as I was, I could figure out how to answer people's disingenuous questions on the network news programs: "How could someone do something like this?"

I knew, also, that by "someone" they meant someone white, someone American. Because when they thought it was a Middle Eastern terrorist, there wasn't this pretending to be baffled.

The answer is simple. Evil begets evil. Atrocity that is allowed to go unanswered will always inspire more atrocity. We pretend we don't know this so we don't have to label our actions as atrocities. There were big laughs on the radio about the "wackos from Waco" who got roasted, just another way of denying humanity so we don't have to think about inhumanity.

I want to blow up a building. But it wouldn't do a goddamn thing.

I dreamt we was all
beautiful and strong

the fullness of him who fills everything in every way
EPHESIANS 1:23

Do not expect too much from the end of the world.
STANISLAW J. LEC

I FELT SOME AMBIVALENCE about moving back to the Midwest during the Trump administration.

It wasn't Trump supporters I was most worried about. I guessed that most of my extended family voted for him, given the Clinton conspiracy theories I'd heard some of them espouse at holiday dinners and the far-right talk-radio hosts I had been subjected to when we stayed over at my aunt's house outside Topeka. I wasn't planning on forcing every person I came into contact with to declare who they had voted for. I assumed the guy in the air force I was fucking had voted for him; I assumed both the bartender and the socialist I was also having sexual relations with had not. I assumed the three frat brothers living next door, whose décor was equal parts guns, Jesus, and Star Wars, had voted for him; I wasn't sure about the gay couple on the other side, who were after all both cops.

I was more worried about people on the coasts, who thought of the middle of the country as newly exotic. "What are they like?" they wanted to know. "You mean my family?" I had heard a twenty-four-year-old Gemini who had recently discovered Marx declare that the answer to all of our problems was a Brooklyn millennial repopulation of the red states: if they were priced out of Bushwick, perhaps they should head to Beloit. There you could buy a four-bedroom house for $55,000, they'd checked the listings. Build a utopia of leftist thought in the high plains, despite not knowing anything about the region. It would be Bleeding Kansas all over again, with an influx of outsiders moving in to influence the vote. Except with bigger guns now. I didn't really think it would work.

Plus, I was tired of Brooklyn. I was tired of Brooklyn when I lived in Brooklyn, and I was tired of Brooklyn when I lived in the parts of Berlin that were becoming Brooklyn. I didn't want it in Kansas too, even if it might bring a short-term advantageous political outcome.

For a minute I almost started to agree with Missouri's new senator, Josh Hawley, when he made a big speech about rootless cosmopolitans. Totally not about Jews, he assured us, despite the use of the well-worn dog whistle. Just the people who consider themselves to be "citizens of the world." They have no loyalty to American values and traditions, he told us. They think of themselves as part of a "global community," prioritizing, I guess, the well-being of the Bangladeshi children making that blouse, not the American H&M shop owner selling it for seven dollars. "The cosmopolitan elite look down on the common affections that once bound this nation together: things like place and national feeling and religious faith. They regard our inherited traditions as oppressive and our shared institutions— like family and neighborhood and church—as backwards."

How could I possibly disagree? I'm in the middle of writing a book about the oppressiveness of the traditions and backwardness of the shared institutions he so dearly values. And I was one of those who naively believed the solution to soulless nationalism was a full embrace of the abundant world. In order to stop Islamophobia, all anyone would have to do is step inside the Blue Mosque in Istanbul. In order to stop hating black people, all they would have to do is meet a black person. In order to stop thinking America is the greatest country on earth, all they would have to do is see Paris, see Buenos Aires, see Nairobi, see Moscow, see Tokyo. But history hasn't borne this theory out. There's a rich tradition of going to another place, seeing people doing things differently, and thinking, "What are all these idiots doing?" whether that be eating cold cuts for breakfast in Germany or kneeling down to pray to a minor variation on the Christian god in the Middle East.

Who gets to go see this wider world? Even when the borders were temporarily thinning, because we were all just so optimistic about cultural exchange, only a small population got across. The well-to-do, the young, the holders of American, British, Australian, and EU passports. They have gone for edification or advancement. Others are forced to go, by circumstance, by poverty, by war, by the need to care for others. But for many, any dreams of a retirement spent in leisurely appreciation of the world went away at the same time dreams of any kind of retirement did. And for many, those dreams never existed at all, because of circumstance, poverty, war, or the need to care for others, and it's an easy thing to resent or suspect people who have access to something that has been denied to you.

It's also easy to get defensive when other people don't value the things you value. Or when you are criticized for loving something that is doing active harm in the world. It makes you cling. Few people are willing to question why they love what they love. Everyone else is crazy for not loving it. They would love it if only they were introduced to it, if only they could be made to see. So why not replicate the whole world with the thing you love? Then there will be so much for you, you'll never have to question anything, and everyone else will be forced to love what you love.

I was ten when I was first exposed to missionary culture. My aunt and uncle were Evangelicals, and going to church with them was at least entertaining. At our local Methodist church, a squat, dark brick cube with a few uninspired stained-glass windows, uncomfortable wooden pews, and a stair lift to raise the infirm—but disappointingly slowly, not at all like the zoom I had first envisioned—sermons were long drones. At the Evangelical church, much brighter and more like a theater than a place of worship, the minister dressed up in robes and thorns and, dripping with fake blood, carried an enormous wooden cross up to the pulpit on Easter Sunday. It was incredible.

But I wasn't converted, because members of their church— like all Evangelical churches its name was a random mix of Holy, Christ, Brotherhood, Light, Christian, something, something— were expected to do more than attend Sunday service. With the Methodists, you show up once a week, if that, maybe drop by the monthly potluck, and all of your god duties are fulfilled. With the Evangelicals, there were constant meetings, prayer groups, reading groups, newsletters, community events, volunteer hours, and interventions. Your whole life became the church. It seemed exhausting.

While we were staying with my aunt and uncle one summer, they took us to meet some missionaries. They were in from Papua New Guinea, and they had sons around my age. They had built a clinic or something, dug wells, whatever, and were back in the States to speak at churches about their experience and to raise funds. They had pictures of their sons standing with bright smiling faces next to natives in traditional dress. They published a regular newsletter, and giving money would get you a subscription. You could read all about their adventures in a strange land with strange people. The whole island, from what I could tell from their presentation, was thatched huts, near-naked men and women, destitution and backwardness.

Of course, they weren't just building clinics and digging wells. They were testifying and converting. They were bringing donations of Western-style clothing for the residents. They were teaching the English language. They were telling the natives about the wonders of Jesus Christ our Lord and Savior. They loved these people, they insisted. They loved the island and its inhabitants and their rituals.

For a while after meeting the missionaries, and being dragged by my aunt and uncle to other meetings and revivals and terrible Christian rock bands, I had thought, what a wonderful way to see the world. You wouldn't just be traveling and experiencing new cultures and foods and horizons, you'd be contributing. It wasn't until my cousins were getting ready for their own missions that I started to question why, if they loved these different places so much, they seemed to want the people they encountered to become just like them.

It's easy to love the world when it reflects back only your face. When it tells only your story. Such a harder, more fragile and exciting thing to love the world for not being you. To not demand that it change for your comfort or pleasure. It means navigating the treacherous wilds between control and moral relativism, between forcing a Bible and a short-sleeve button-down shirt on everyone in the world and waving your hands uselessly, saying, "who are we to judge?" when a community executes a gay man or cuts off the external sexual organs of a teenage girl or sends emissaries into another country to force its residents into baptism.

So much harder to treat the world as a garden. To weed rather than raze. To nurture rather than handle. To compost rather than pave over. To encourage rather than twist. To suggest rather than insist. To tend rather than master. To encourage variety rather than monoculture. To allow frivolity instead of utility. To observe and delight rather than intervene. To be humble and questioning rather than certain.

I, of course, was always one of their projects, someone to convert and save. All the heathens in the family would get the same Christian propaganda from my aunt and uncle, and it only stopped when I stopped going back. But a few years ago, I was accidentally included on an appeal for funds for my cousin's mission to South East Asia.

I called my mother. "Does he even speak the language?"

"No. I think he's going to teach English through the church."

"This is the dumbest thing I've ever heard."

But he wasn't much different from other cousins who joined the military, who went overseas to reshape the world, not with a Bible and some introductory English lessons, but with a gun. Or a drone, I guess, is what they use now.

As a child, I was lectured to by Christians about how people should be. Not some people, just people. Respectable. God-fearing. They should wear khaki pants if men, floral blouses and skirts if women. They should speak English. They should proselytize. They should marry young to someone of the opposite sex, and they should have many children. They should be prosperous and treat their house and family as if it were a fortress. If people didn't know this is how a person should live, they should be treated with pity. If people did know this is how a person should live yet lived in a different way, they should be treated with scorn.

As a teenager, I was lectured to by men of authority, like my father and my minister and my teachers, about how people should be. Not some people, just people. They told me there couldn't be economic equality because there's no true human equality. Some people are just better than others, and as such they should be rewarded. And you can't just give money to the lessers, because how do you know they won't waste it? You need competition to inspire greatness. No one would invent anything or create anything or do a chore like picking up the garbage if they didn't have to do it to survive. They saw all people the way they saw themselves, as selfish, as incapable of grace, as living their lives as an act of spiteful survival and not of joy. If people didn't behave as they dictated, they were to be kept in a state of deprivation until they shaped up, or slipped and were sent to prison, or died.

Now as an adult, I am lectured to by socialists, leftists, people younger than me about how people should be. Not some people, just people. People need to speak and think in a very specific way. They should only enjoy and create very specific works of art, and all other works of art should be condemned if not outright destroyed. They believe people are equal, but that equality necessarily means speaking, thinking, reading, fucking, spending money, dressing in one very specific way. People who do not conform can't possibly have not read the rules—it must be that they are dangerous. Dangerous people are subject to removal from positions of authority and from public life.

They are all missionaries. Salvation is guaranteed if you follow their strict guidelines. I get it. You want to be treated in a certain way, but you can't be certain that treatment will come to you naturally, so you want to enforce and control it. You want the world to be kind and accepting, but you know from experience that isn't always the case. So rather than be kind and accepting yourself, and be taken for some kind of rube, you want to legislate a certain type of behavior that mimics kindness and acceptance.

It's not just kindness. I've listened to socialists tell me that after the "revolution" women will be freed from things like cosmetics and dresses. I've listened to Christians say that when the kingdom of heaven rules on earth trans men and women will find peace in their biological bodies. I've listened to Republicans say that once they gain full control of the government, women will be liberated from abortion to find satisfaction in motherhood. I've listened to feminists say when true gender equality is established, men will be free from toxic masculinity and admit they like shopping and reject hobbies like sports.

There is a reason the cosmopolitan is seen as a threat, and not just to Missouri senators. Not cosmopolitan in the sense of the couple who took a cruise to Venice, on the kind of ship that will ensure Venice almost certainly disappears in another generation or two, and now think they've seen Italy. Nor do I mean the bros who developed an app during a yoga retreat in Bali, during which they managed never to be in a room with an Indonesian. Nor the twenty-two-year-old with avant-garde bangs who works in a gallery in Berlin and has never had a conversation longer than a coffee order with someone who does not self-identify as an artist or a curator. I mean the cosmopolitan who is accepting and enthusiastic about the multiplicity of ideas, beliefs, modes of being, ways of living, gender expressions, and breakfast foods available in the world. They don't see an unspoiled prairie and fantasize about building a artists' retreat for burned-out Brooklynites there. They don't see a woman in a headscarf and feel compelled to tell her she doesn't have to live that way. They might assist in creating an environment where flourishing is possible, but they don't have a strict definition of what flourishing looks like. Other than it not being where one group chokes out another.

I've met a lot of cosmopolitans in my day. I've met them in dive bars in Lawrence, Kansas, and in tavernas in Athens, Greece. They've been my bosses and people I've met in passing. I've gotten drunk with them, read their books, listened to their music, seen their art. It has nothing to do with their race, their gender, their age. It has nothing to do with how much of the world they've seen or which university they went to. It's in their temperament. They don't make assumptions that because of your race, your gender, your age you will be a certain way or live a certain kind of life. They're curious and willing to meet you as you are. They tolerate strangeness.

The reason cosmopolitans are a threat is that in their presence you can allow yourself to be strange. You don't have to hold yourself so rigidly, you don't have to anticipate rejection or misunderstanding. You don't have to smile politely to keep a snarl in check when they ask you when you're going to start having kids, when they ask about your family or church or political party, when they start telling you your own story. You can unspool yourself. You don't have to pretend like you're conforming—or aggressively prove that you're different. You can just be, because your specialness is acknowledged, just like that of the guy farther down the bar, even though he is just some cis fucking guy in a baseball cap drinking a cheap beer. You can feel yourself becoming cosmopolitan in their presence. Their goodness is contagious.

They are a threat because they are going to care about harm done to people, even those who don't look like them or live in the same locale. They will not tolerate being told that the harm is being done for their own benefit or comfort. They won't believe you when you assert what is best for them or how they should be, because they already know.

Cosmopolitans are inherently ungovernable, because they work by morals and not by laws. They are loyal to people, not to structures. They will not automatically acknowledge your authority just because you have a badge or a degree or a suit. You have to prove that those declarative sentences you are throwing at them are valid.

It's not about external expressions of sophistication, the "oh this? I got it in Rome," the French epigraph for their autobiographical novel, their internationally adopted children, the vinyl collection "because I just prefer the real thing, you know?" It's an emotional sophistication. It's a sophistication that isn't stripped away when your possessions are not around.

For a couple of days, it looked like Kanye West was going to run for president. In what was maybe a manic episode, he announced via social media and public appearances that he wanted to be the next president of the United States. And I thought, yeah, okay, sure, why not?

As I write this, we have a president who brags about his ability to walk down stairs and drink a glass of water with one hand, and we have a Democratic challenger who falls asleep on live television, so I am having a hard time thinking it would be terrible if Kanye West usurped them both to occupy the Oval Office. He is sincerely a musical genius, and he also designed some good pants. If he can produce an album as great as *My Dark Twisted Fantasy*, is it too much of a stretch to imagine he can produce a health care policy of the same quality?

For years, we have been in essence functioning without a

government. Our president issues some insane edict, like only classical architecture for new federal buildings or canceling our health insurance, and we all have to find ways to survive it. Our local governments give free rein to police unions and property developers, and we have to try to live our lives with a little dignity anyway. Our federal legislature might as well not exist; they couldn't even find a way to distribute a stimulus package in the early days of the pandemic that wasn't like a big cash drop from a helicopter, some of us walking away with a fist full of dollars and others wondering what the hell just happened. At every level, our government is failing to maintain an environment where people can be sustainably housed, fed, paid, and cared for.

So when I say we are functioning, I'm not saying we're doing a great job, what with the mass death and the extremely long lines at food pantries and the eviction crisis and the wilding out at grocery stores, but we are not all yet dead and for that I am truly proud of us.

Maybe it would help, then, to make it official and abolish the presidency. Or not abolish it, exactly. Just remove all the office's powers. We need a place to store our megalomaniacs, after all. There is a certain type of person who will always think, you know what, the world should be better, and I'm just the person to do it, and then they go about improving things by deporting children, starving children, drone-bombing children, poisoning children. We need to give them a space and an office and some business cards that make them feel as important as they need to be reassured they are, and every once and a while we can gather together and clap at the things they say so they don't try to murder us or murder other people on our behalf. It'll be ceremonial, like the queen of England. And like the queen, we'll let Kanye wear a nice hat and we'll pretend we care about the goings-on of his children and he'll go to other countries to have his photo taken with other world leaders and we'll let him sit in the best seats at polo games and so on.

But, I hear you protesting, who will decide which Middle Eastern country to invade on false pretenses? Who will rearrange the tax code every couple of years into another bizarre and confusing configuration? Who will give pep talks to the very stressed and disrespected Wall Street bankers without whom we would have a much nicer world and maybe some local newspapers, thank you very much?

We are in a moment of toppling statues, a moment of recognizing that the people we have been taught to revere aren't actually worth aspiring to be like. That actually, a lot of those guys should have been doing something else with their time, like instead of writing one dumb and random document from which our entire conception of what a government should be and do, they should have taken up woodworking. Sure, every once and a while you get a Lincoln or a Jesus or a Kanye, but for the most part, the promise of power attracts the wicked and the useless, the egotistically frail and the spiritually broken. Instead of just throwing someone new at the office every couple of years, hoping this one won't secretly hate black people, maybe we should rethink letting one person have that much influence over how the world works.

Among the most beautiful by-products of the Trump years are the sincere expressions of wanting to help. No, I don't want you to die because you don't have insulin; here, stranger, have some of the money I was going to spend on tacos. No, actually, I don't think you should sit in jail during a pandemic because you moved your arm a little near a cop so have been arrested for resisting arrest; have some bail money. The outpouring of donations to nonprofits, GoFundMes, bail funds, mutual aid funds, food banks, and other charities has shown that, for the most part, we do want to take care of each other. So let's find better, smarter, more efficient ways of doing that, even if it means moving some of the government's powers and not letting it interfere so much.

I want a world of flourishing, where flourishing is defined as something other than never being questioned or argued with, never encountering difference, having the ability to take up as much space as I please.

I had a garden once. It was dominated by what I called the demon bush, which was actually a large tangle of plants, including a maple tree, poison ivy, and other assorted nasties. In the summer something in this mess would bloom with white flowers that smelled like heaped-up trash bags and called to flies to pollinate them so the demon bush could continue to self-replicate. I was always tying it back, hacking it to bits, but the root system went all through the garden, and as I pulled on one root I could never tell which terrible part of the tangle I was chasing. Every fall I would feel like I had made some progress on diminishing it, but come spring, the demon bush would erupt yet again.

Yes, this is a metaphor.

I managed to plant around it. I had berry bushes, and the blackberry with its mighty root system did much to block the growth of the demon bush. I had less hacking to do, and the smells of the garden weren't overpowered by the dumpster stench. I had all kinds of herbs—if you had an unwanted pregnancy, I had things to help deal with that—and I started to plant roses, foxglove, and heather.

I was teaching myself, learning from books which types of plants liked which type of conditions, and then I worked to create those conditions for those plants. The sage was so happy I had to prune it back and start using it in almost everything I cooked. I soaked my tampons in the watering can and used that to feed the roses; the roses bloomed wildly. Some things didn't work. The radishes never did amount to much, and the comfrey got so ecstatic it blocked the light to the tansy. Others would seem to die off, then burst back to life two years later. I got used to treating the plants as they wanted to be treated. And when I moved away from that house, I only really mourned the garden. Well, that and the way, when I woke up at 4 a.m. with my habitual insomnia, my bed jammed up against the window, I had only to open my eyes to see a sky full of stars.

When I moved to Kansas City, I went about trying to recreate the garden. I set up a compost pile, which a possum named Harriet would root around in almost every night at dusk. I dug up vines that had choked out almost everything else in the yard. I delicately picked out bits of broken glass from the soil, along with nails, bits of wood, paint chips, and trash.

But there was something wrong with the soil. Or the energy of the place—maybe it was the ghost stomping out my attempts to enjoy the space. Within seconds of going outside I was swarmed with mosquitoes, and no amount of poison sprayed on my skin would deter them. I planted rhubarb, and some animal (or ghost) ripped the plant out of the ground the next night. The black walnut tree in the back was trying to recreate itself over and over again, killing off any diversity of flora. My raspberry bush died. My hydrangeas turned brown within twelve hours of planting. What looked like fecundity, because the backyard was green and lush, was just a mess of hostile invaders that refused to cede territory, refused to share.

Yes, this is also a metaphor. But now I know how to repair soil. I know when to start mixing in manure or compost, seaweed or straw. I also know when it's best to simply cover the toxic ground with an impermeable layer and lay good soil on top of it. Let the land rest for a while. Plant things that don't need to go so deep, that will sit pleasantly on the surface, allowing the mysterious processes of recovery to continue beneath. It's still going.

The path of error

DAD THREE

THE GOD

Martin Luther

Part of the terror is to take back our own listening. To use our own voice. To see our own light.

HILDEGARD VON BINGEN

Asked if he believed in God, he said Yes, and asked what it meant to believe in God, he answered that it meant eating well, drinking well, and getting up at 10 o'clock in the morning.

HENRY KAMEN, *THE SPANISH INQUISITION*

THE METHODIST CHURCH WAS LIKE the Presbyterian church was like the Lutheran church was like the Episcopalian church. We went to the Methodist church because it was the church my father was confirmed into as a child, but it might as well have been because it was two blocks from our house. Maybe my father was confirmed into the Methodist church in Tecumseh, Kansas, because it was only four blocks from his childhood home.

Sometimes we would go to the Presbyterian church. They did crossover events, and there didn't seem to be much of a difference between this church and our church. The ministers wore the same nondescript business preacher outfits. The sermons were essentially the same. All the same characters were involved. Samson and his hair, Daniel and his lions, the Samaritan woman and her well. The songs were essentially the same, "Onward Christian Soldiers" and "Morning Has Broken" and all the others, all sung listlessly, standing rigidly, with no emotion at all. And the people were essentially the same, just a slightly different sampling of the teachers, farmers, nurses, waitresses, and business owners who barely populated the town. Why couldn't we go to this church instead? The building was nicer, a peaked limestone structure rather than the squat redbrick square of our church, with its narrow stairways and the basement with the decades-old wall-to-wall green carpeting that smelled like the load of laundry you forget in the machine for a week, and when you discover it, you dump in an overflowing cup of detergent, crank it to high, and hope that will rid your clothes of the pinpricks of green-brown mildew and the smell of damp and hidden rot.

But even in a nicer building, it was all the same to me. I mostly spent the service drawing on the programs. As long as we kept quiet and didn't pinch our sister, and looked somewhat like we were paying attention, we were allowed to read or draw. But when I asked why we couldn't just go to whatever church, I was told it was because this was our church and our community. We're Methodists.

This was before the storefront churches started opening, nondenominational and filled with folding chairs and card tables. This was before the megachurches started opening an hour's drive away, where they'd tell attendees God wanted them to be rich and that it was okay to sway when you sing and to close your eyes and put your hands up in the air and feel things, but only certain things.

When I was a teenager, my aunt took me to revivals. I would be saved, again and again and again. With the music swelling and the whole arena swaying and the preacher intoning, "Come be seen by God," I would start weeping. I would feel saved, I would feel blessed. I would be entirely overcome by the presence of God. The preacher would ask those who were ready to let Jesus into their hearts to announce themselves, to come to the front of the room. I would come.

But then they'd take you in the back and try to minister to

you. They would try to explain the experience you were having, and they were always wrong. Moved by the Holy Spirit, sure, but now there were all sorts of rules. Now I was expected to hold hands with this stranger who would pray for me without even asking what I might want out of this. He would ask the Lord to come into my heart and clear out the darkness. He would assume he knew what this darkness was.

I would keep going for the feeling, but then I would skip the ministering. Having sobbed wildly in a room full of other sobbers and wailers and swayers, I would leave with my cousins and pretend I felt nothing. It was a relief to have a collective feeling, to be overwhelmed and yet held. To have a space to leave all of that feeling and be able to walk away from it, rather than having it become a chore, something I had to think about and talk about and be talked to about.

The revivals had something that the regular Sunday services didn't: immediacy. I didn't understand why we couldn't just stay in that moment of revelation every week. I know other people have jobs, and it's hard to do algebra homework or do data entry or pay your taxes when you're carrying around an ecstatic encounter, but still. The rest of it, the sermons and the bad songs, seemed unnecessary in the face of the possibility for holy fire.

I'm always looking to recreate those feelings, that big collective cry, the separation between bodies and emotions finally falling away, the space to fill with your sobbing, with your grief, with your spiritual longing, with the feelings that are too big for one corporeal form, to just release it all into the air to mingle with everyone else's and then walk away from it. I've looked for it in movie theaters, at the opera, in Tori Amos concerts. I've envied men weeping in each other's arms at sporting events.

Only once did I find that feeling in an actual church. I stood in a tiny medieval church in Bucharest, the ceiling low, a thick gloom with candlelight filtered through incense smoke. The walls were covered in very old murals, creepy and fantastical paintings of unsettling angels. Not the beatific creatures of romantic imaginations, they were as fearsome and disturbing as an encounter with the divine must be. I couldn't understand the language, but nuns in smart little hats and dark shrouds sang unearthly sounds. I swayed, I was overcome, I cried. I lost my breath and had to step outside, the closest exit led me to a walled garden filled with roses and plum trees full of fruit.

I want to exist only in that space. That church, that garden. To travel only between the dark mysteries of the soul and the sunlit fecundity of the earth. Nothing else, only these two extremes, I want to run back and forth between them for the rest of my life.

The Methodist church was founded during a revivalist moment, a moment when Christians looked around, saw their churches were no longer satisfactory, were not interpreting the Bible the right way, had deviated from the original Christian principles as this new generation understood them. They would invent a new church, more in line with the first teachings of Christ, to get Christianity back on track.

John Wesley looked around the eighteenth-century Christian landscape and saw some issues. Calvinist predestination was too influential a force. The church had strayed from its original principles of poverty and simplicity. Wesley thought there was no need for so much theological fussing, that the true revelations could all be found in the original holy text, the Bible. There was a need for a new direction, by which he meant an old direction, one more aligned with original intentions. The Methodist church was established based mostly on Wesley's ideas of those original intentions.

He was splitting off from Martin Luther, who had looked around the sixteenth-century Christian landscape and seen some issues. The Catholic Church had too tight a hold over its people. It had strayed from its original principles of a direct relationship with God, and he rejected the greed the church showed in its selling of indulgences and its bestowing, or withholding, of the sacraments. There was a need for a new direction, by which he meant an old direction, one more aligned with original intentions. The great Reformation was enacted, based mostly on Luther's ideas of those original intentions.

Since Wesley, there have been groups within the Methodist church who examined how the church was functioning and what it was teaching and saw some issues. There was either too much emphasis on mysticism and speaking in tongues or not enough. There was either too much talk of equality, particularly as it involved women and African Americans in the United States, or not enough. Groups created different splinter churches and sects, churches more aligned with their ideas of Christianity's original intentions.

Even then, with Protestantism splintered into a thousand shards, there were individuals and groups who looked around the twentieth-century Christian landscape and saw some issues. There were too many intermediaries, too many interpretations. Each of these critics read the original holy text and believed they had discerned its original intention. And each founded a church, one that said you shouldn't go to the doctor, one that said blood transfusions are like eating blood, one that said we should have monks again but without the Catholicism, one that said you should pay for the preacher's cosmetic dental work and new car and pool and Florida mansion and prostitutes, one that said we should ask ghosts things, one that said the world was going to end and we were all about to be raptured, another that said the world was going to end and a select few would be saved by UFOs, another that said we should all be vegetarians, and another where everyone either drank poison or got shot in the head. Each one insisted it had the right way of interpreting Christ's message and the right way of behaving and worshipping God. All the other ones were wrong.

All of this splintering, all of this backtracking and forward-tracking and sidetracking, all of this interpretation and reinter-pretation, all of this restoration and reinvention and config-uring and reconfiguring, it is not proof of Christianity's great creativity. It's not proof of its durability or universality. It's not proof of its great power to meet people where they live or to show them great answer to their questions and their problems. If anything, it just shows how well the church tracks with our shopping habits. Everyone is always finding a new way to turn God into a gimmick, complete with a new ad campaign and updated formula.

The fact that Christ's original teachings can be used to say, somehow, both that one should embrace poverty and that one should get as rich as possible because cash is how God bestows blessings, both that all people are equal and the marginalized, the judged, and the demonized should be embraced and that we should marginalize, judge, and demonize anyone we don't agree with, that's proof we are moving further and further away from the basic teachings, that all churches have corrupted and twisted and misinterpreted some aspect of Christ's thoughts.

And doesn't that make you want to start a new church? One that goes back to those original principles that everyone else is so thick about? Or maybe to go further back, invent a religion or a church that bypasses patriarchy altogether by "rediscovering" a matriarchal culture lost to time? You could dig up some stone carvings or jewelry that has lost all meaning and context and invent new ones to support your fantasy about a time in which everything was better. Or invent an egalitarian culture also lost to time. Or jump forward to the future and invent a religion based on aliens and fuzzy concepts about space travel.

But your followers will just fuck it up. Or your descendants. Or your cofounder, in a decades-long power struggle. A generation from now, everyone will misinterpret what you're saying, and no one will bother to get out a Ouija board and ask you how you feel about it. If I Ouija'd John Wesley right now and asked him how he felt about the church services I attended in his name, with a man in polyester pants up there in the pulpit telling us that man is the head of the household and the wife is necessarily subservient to him, if I told him about the potluck with macaroni salad with cheese cubes and frozen peas or the cherry crumble that is just a can of mushy cherries in hyperactively sweet slop with some sugary oatmeal dumped on top, he would lose his goddamn mind. He would start pacing back and forth in that church basement as a half-seen apparition and never find rest again.

I actually like John Wesley, kind of. He was an abolitionist and a feminist, kind of. He believed in poverty and simplicity, and he thought God was as likely to be found outdoors as in a church. There seemed to be less scolding about behavior. It wasn't do this, don't do this incessantly, it was helping people to find the core of their beliefs as a means of aligning their actions with their sense of right and wrong. But I never found Wesley in the church services I attended involuntarily.

Left to my own devices, had I been able to choose a church that suited my needs, I probably would have been Catholic.

They had the only nice church in my town. It felt very mysterious, with the holy water and the confessionals and the honest-to-god *outfits*. And as someone whose temperament runs to excess, the idea of an intermediary, someone to tell me I'm going to hell or I'm not going to hell, this is a sin or this is not a sin, would have been tempting at various times in my life. But then, as someone whose temperament runs toward the anti-authoritarian, I probably would have rejected the priest's interpretations, or at least argued endlessly until he told me that yes, I was definitely going to hell, now please get out of my church.

And maybe my sense that I knew best would have led me to the Evangelicals, who like to tell people that the ultimate authority on what god means is just you; even if you're a big idiot who can't work a can opener, you get to decide what God wants from all of us. But then, they were all so embarrassingly earnest and sweet and with polo shirts two sizes too big tucked into pleated khakis and belted. That still might have flown until they told me to live god's truth by ministering to others, when I think that mostly people would like to be left alone, so then maybe I would have wandered over to the Unitarians.

My sense is, I could have wasted a lot of years trying to find the right church, the right external expression of my internal sense of god, morality, and the infinite. Because it's there, like a bird trapped in a house, flapping its wings frantically against the clean window, not sure why it can't turn glass into air.

The Kansas territory needed white settlers right around the time European radicals needed homes. The revolutions of 1848, which stretched all across the continent and, while not united in organization, were united in their vision of overthrowing aristocratic control, sent many into exile. It was mostly Northern Europeans—Swedes, Danes, Germans—who settled on the

Midwestern plains, bringing their Protestant beliefs along with their families and few possessions. This is more or less when my own family reached the region, although we have more oppressors than oppressed in our lineage.

And the white radicals of the European lower classes who had been thrown from their homes by the oligarchic ruling class now fought for their place on land that until recently had belonged to Native American tribes thrown from their homes by the oligarchic ruling class, because that is how things go. The solution to your own persecution always seems to be to put yourself in a position to persecute others.

The simplicity of the setting suits the faith. Just as there is nothing between you and the weather that will destroy your livelihood as a farmer or rancher, there are no institutions between you and your god. No buffer, no intermediary, no one to intercede on your behalf when it's clear that he's pissed at you and you don't know why. No need for an ornate cathedral—a simple stone or wood structure will do, a beauty as timidly grand as the wind rushing through the tall grasses as they sway and dance. Or whatever.

As a result, there has never been a significant population of Catholics in Kansas. Despite the varying names—Lutheran, Methodist, Presbyterian, some Mennonites over to the side—the churches were all pretty much the same, in that they were all created out of the tantrums of Martin Luther. The rise of the Evangelicals took Luther's worst ideas and amplified them. And for some reason, Kansas became a place where variations on the theme kept getting spat out. New branches of an old faith originate here, from the Pentecostals to splinter groups like Zion Valley, as does the widening divide between Protestants and Evangelicals.

The idea that the Reformation freed believers from superstition and domination prevailed. Catholics were not to be trusted, because they lacked the capacity for reason. They were constantly looking to someone else, a priest or even the pope, to tell them what to do. And didn't the Reformation liberate women? Weren't nuns essentially captives, poor deluded women cut off from the glorious experiences of sex, desire, motherhood, marriage, and family?

But freedom is often hubris. Can an individual deal with god all on his own? Absolutely fucking not, or at least that's what thousands of years of practice had told us. Up until Luther said, no, go ahead, read the book on your own, decide what it means, talk to him directly, decide in your own brain what is a sin, what is a prayer, what is proper penance, what is obedience, what is an honest and devoted life.

Calling that freedom seems ridiculous. It means carrying god around with you all day, every day. There is no place to put him. He swarms, he engulfs. The lines between this world and the next blur.

It presupposes the idea that people want to be or are better off liberated from superstition and guides, that they prefer simplicity over decadence, that ideology is always swallowed whole, or even that there is a nonsuperstitious form of Christianity when we're all sitting here pretending this wine tastes like blood.

It also presupposes the idea that the function of religion is to determine what is good and bad behavior, what god wants from us, so that we can then live in alignment with god's will. Rather than managing the relationship between the human and the divine, providing a framework of meaning, and helping people move through symbol and metaphor to ritualize the natural world and our role within it and find a way to understand our own mortality. That might sound like the same thing, but it's really not.

The way many write about the Reformation, one might assume the people of the church, the actual believers and parishioners and lay people, felt liberated by the changes it effected. One might assume they had been crying out for such changes, unable to shake things up themselves because of the tight control the church had over them. One might assume the women of the church—the nuns and so on—would gleefully rip off their habits and burn them in giant pyres, finally freed from oppression.

Some welcomed the changes, sure. But the Reformation was also experienced as a trauma. Churches were suddenly denuded of the artwork that had meant so much to so many. The rituals of the liturgical calendar, feast days and fast days and festival days and days of this offering or that prayer, were gone. Mary's position as a goddess figure was attacked. And the monasteries and convents, among other structures, were gone. States decided their citizens' religions for them, forcing those who wanted to worship in a different way to emigrate, breaking up families and communities and entire cities.

In the decades before the Reformation, people were indeed crying out. They were crying out for infrastructure, weary from having so many of the people they knew and loved killed by wave after wave of disease. They were crying out for liberation from high taxes, most of which were levied to fight wars that might change their leader but not the conditions under which they lived. They wanted to empty out the jails, tired of being harassed by the powerful when trying to live their lives. They were less likely to be freaking out over different theories about transubstantiation, unless whipped into it by radical preachers.

And the issues they did have with the church would not necessarily be addressed by the Reformation. That the Lutheran church wouldn't sell indulgences didn't mean it wouldn't find new ways to exploit its followers or fill them with dread about the afterlife. In fact, it invented wholly new ways to freak people out about the afterlife, like inventing the idea of predestination, telling people that no matter how they behaved they were probably going to burn in hell.

What Luther was trying to do was to bring Christianity into better alignment with prophecy about Armageddon. If the church operated more as instructed in the Bible's descriptions of the Last Days, then we could bring about the end of the world. In other words, Luther is just another one of these guys who would rather see the world destroyed because it disappoints him than work through the trouble and try to generate new life, new ideas, and new structures. I am so very tired of people who want the world to burn.

Right now there are Protestants who support the state of Israel in the hopes that its control of a prescribed territory will bring back the Messiah, and the ensuing war between heaven and hell will kill most of us. But they will find a renewed kingdom of peace when it's all over, so it's probably worth the human rights violations, the apartheid state, the physical occupation, the daily humiliations and assertions of dominance, the random killings of activists and intellectuals and doctors by snipers, that the actual state of Israel lives by and through.

Does that mean Christianity itself is just another apocalyptic death cult, hurtling toward oblivion because the world is too hard? Or that everyone out to destroy the world is simply living out their Christian teachings, whether or not they, at this moment or any other, believe in god? Built into the idea of the birth of the world in Christianity is a plan for its destruction—

not only a plan but a very sincere wish. It's not surprising for a religion that positioned itself against the earth rather than as a part of it. But it means that to solve the riddle of the father and the country, one also must untangle the god who created them.

Why Luther? When I read his biography, I have a hard time arguing with him. He supported a separation between church and state, and he believed in a secular legal system rather than one built around Christian law. He thought ostentatious wealth was a sin. He thought financial systems that charged interest went against god, and he believed the power of corporations should be curbed. He did not believe everyone needed to adopt asceticism or deprivation or the life of the monk. He did not believe Christians should be beholden to any religious authority other than god. He believed that a union with Christ was enough to redeem individuals and allow them to navigate the world with a lightness of spirit and conscience.

And if that had been the world he had created, if that had been the kind of world I was born into, it would have been good. But he managed to put into motion systems that do just the opposite of everything he taught. The Protestant faith would soon turn into a religion of prosperity, and his believers become hypercorporate in their mindset.

How can we come to terms with the distance between what people say and what they do? Or the distance between what one person writes and what another person reads? Luther supported the position of the peasant, and yet he contributed to their oppression. And many of his students and readers took his words about the dignity of work and the devotion of labor and used them to insist on their rights as landlords and managers.

In today's Evangelical movement, one sees Luther's inconsistent hand in everything. This verse that says gays are an abomination is extremely important. This other verse that says the Israelites were held as slaves in Egypt, even though that contradicts the written record and almost certainly did not happen, well, that's a metaphor. This other verse that says turn the other cheek is basically not even there; God definitely wants us to have guns and protect our property.

In some churches, the story of the Samaritan is interpreted as meaning we should welcome migrants and refugees with open arms. In others, that we should protect our borders, with weapons if necessary. Some interpret Jesus's teachings to mean that Christians should embrace poverty; others believe the same verses mean God bestows prosperity on the worthy.

Martin Luther stressed the need for the Bible to be translated into vernacular language, made available so that all could read god's teachings directly. He wanted people to see the book for themselves and not rely on the interpretations of a church or a priest who could warp the meaning of the words to fit their own ill intentions. Everyone warps the meaning of words to fit their own ill intentions, even if only unconsciously.

The Evangelicals at the church my aunt used to take me to loved to say that the word of god was the truth. But religion isn't about truth, it's about meaning, and somehow that was forgotten along the way. And meaning isn't something external, it's an interaction between the internal and the external. It's a constant act of creation, not a place on which to stand. It's dynamic and shifting, and exciting and dangerous.

One book is not enough to create meaning. Our brains are dumb, filled with a lifelong accumulation of lies, advertisements, superhero movies, recipes for pot roast, poorly remembered lyrics from songs heard on the radio back when there was radio, books we read when we were too young to understand, very important thoughts about a dress we saw at the mall, specific preferences for coffee and cake, half-constructed philosophical systems, the thing we read on Twitter earlier today, an image from a dream two years ago, every single episode of a television show that ran for seven years that we watched three times, seventy-two nicknames for our cat, today's horoscope, and a YouTube video of a porcupine eating a pumpkin that we think about four times a day. I'm supposed to take that whole jumble and synthesize it with the holy word of god?

Meaning isn't created through language alone. And the festivals, the feasts and fasts, the liturgical calendar, the artwork, the music, the feeling of being in a room filled with incense and whispered voices, is all part of the creation of meaning. Because meaning is not just about the rational brain, which will think whatever it wants to think. It's the unconscious that controls the religious experience, and it's been shut out of the proceedings.

Luther admonished the iconoclasts, saying no, don't go into churches and smash the faces off of Jesus, that's weird. Just destroy them in your mind. "When they are no longer in the heart, they can do no harm when seen with the eyes." But a lot of people just wanted to destroy them with hammers, not with their heart. If the images were as bad as Luther said, then their interpretation was that they should no longer exist.

Luther seems to have created meaning through Christianity mostly through his use of language. A former monk, he emphasized reading and learning and thinking and speaking. He could get to the "truest" expression of God through only the word itself, so he presumed that was the best way for everyone to create meaning through religion. He held to this belief even after he saw a bunch of people interpret his words in ways he hadn't intended and then run off and do something stupid because of it.

He saw people making meaning through things other than words, like art and festivals and rituals and prayers to saints and parades and baked goods, and he thought they were all doing it wrong. Their meaning can't be the same as my meaning because it looks different. He didn't just shrug and disagree; he argued for the destruction of those things, to keep people's attention on the right ways of making meaning. A bunch of young men agreed with him—and it always seems to be young men—and went about doing the destroying.

I keep finding myself on the brink of arguing that things used to be better and we should go back to that better time. We should reestablish traditions. We should excavate what remains and recreate what has been lost. Bring back the liturgical calendar. Bring back the feasts and the fasts. Bring back the old saints, or even the old gods. Let's all go stand in the woods and worship a tree or dig a big pit and sacrifice our children or turn city parks into temples and dance in ecstatic orgies.

But every attempt to return to tradition somehow ends in nationalism or fundamentalism. It only really appeals to the very literal-minded, a small group of weirdos insisting we all join in on something we don't understand. And enforcing their beliefs with violence if necessary. The reason it never works is because, not only have the traditions been lost, the shared meaning is gone. Our common language, symbols, and imaginations are different now. It's not the act of coming together and lighting candles and eating saffron buns and wearing white robes with red sashes that made St. Lucy's feast day special. It's the metaphor represented by celebrating light on the darkest night of the year, to remind us that time moves on, that things change, that it's possible to find and create little sparks in the blackest despair. That's the power. Forcing a young girl into a robe and shoving a wreath onto her head isn't going to help her feel that power, because the meaning wasn't passed down. The tradition was interrupted. The inheritance was lost.

That doesn't mean we should all throw up our hands and live only in the rational mindset, which is what the New Atheists tried to convince us of a while back. They were following Luther, too, but swapping out a scientific formula for the holy word.

No, it means we should come together to create new forms of shared meaning. New ways of representing the things we lack. Of those there are many.

Eventually, the feelings evoked by the revivals were not enough to keep me interested in Christianity. My Sunday school teacher's political lectures gnawed at me. I started arguing with my parents about having to go, and my father told me, "Don't let people you disagree with keep you from something that means something to you."

But this was a church that had betrayed me; I did not betray it. This was a church that told me my teacher was in hell for killing himself. This was a church that had told me (and Shirley Pianalto) that the father was the head of the house and the representative of God and must be obeyed. This was a church that tried to tell me what to think politically, which was none of its business. This was a church that condemned my friends who were gay, who had sex before marriage, who had abortions or listened to heavy metal or fell into addiction. The church betrayed its own authority, and I didn't leave it, it left me.

That was when I realized the Protestant faith didn't mean much to me. The stories of the Bible did not move me, the music and the service and the community didn't move me, Jesus's sacrifice didn't move me, because what does it even mean to die for my sins, I didn't ask for that and please don't try to tell me Jesus died because I liked to put my hands down my pants, really, please, grow up. I sat, enduring all of it, trying not to look at the clock, thinking, if I delay looking at the clock then when I do look at the clock so much time will have passed and I will be surprised at how close we are to the end, I guess I can look now it seems it's been so long, oh no. Meanwhile, I had an enormous hunger for some sort of connection that wasn't being met. I started to experiment.

Because I was the type of teen to dye my hair black and express my dissatisfaction by forcing everyone in the house to hear muffled Hole records coming through my slammed-shut bedroom door, I got into Wicca. Surely this was what I was needing. I was a *feminist* or whatever, so it felt freeing to reject the monotheistic patriarchal Yahweh. I loved drama, so getting to wear a cloak and burn candles was exciting.

There had been exactly three books about Wicca at the bookshop in the Salina, Kansas, mall. Each had an unappealing pastel cover, with a woman in a shapeless gown and a beatific smile, something better suited to the front of a box of tampons than to a theologically rigorous treatise. Gone was the black pentagram of earlier decades, conjuring thoughts of death metal and sweet transgression. This was the 1990s, the tail end of the Satanic Panic, and the esoteric religions were trying to rebrand as something more grounded in nature and femininity. They were trying to distinguish themselves both from the patriarchal religions and the splinter group of Satanists; in doing so they leaned a bit too heavily on crystals and incense and mother goddess nonsense.

My interest didn't last. I thought it would be better to worship a goddess. I thought if everyone worshipped a goddess as well as a god, we would have a much better world. I thought if we incorporated nature into the sphere of worship, we'd stop dumping our plastic and styrofoam everywhere. I thought if we embraced sorority rather than hierarchy, we could move through the world with fewer power imbalances and learn to see each other as equals rather than rivals or subordinates.

I got all three books despite the deeply embarrassing cover art. I saved up for candles, eventually settling for vanilla-scented tapers from Duckworth's because that's all they had. I bought a deck of tarot cards and started to have opinions about the fact that my sun was in Cancer. I drew my circles, I talked to the moon—but I was always kind of doing that anyway—and I waited for the magic to come. All of this coincided with my first connection to the internet, a long-distance dial-up connected to the computer in our kitchen. After my parents went to bed, I explored Wiccan bulletin boards. Here were the enlightened people I'd been searching for, the ones who would help create a fairer world through feminine divinity.

What I found was—of course—complaints about specific men within the pagan community who had been raping or sexually assaulting or pressuring young women into "sex magick" they didn't want to do. I found male-dominated covens and men refusing to question or give up their power. I found men refusing to give their wives credit when they collaborated on books or art. I found the patriarchy I had been hoping to escape.

I also found splinter groups. There was an original pagan group, and a different coven with a slightly different interpretation of spellwork that had broken off from that, and then another group that broke away from that one because they disagreed on the design of the rituals. It was the fragmenting of Protestantism I had been hoping to escape.

Plus it all felt so made-up. Despite claims of a direct lineage to ancient matriarchal cults, it was just a couple decades old, mostly developed by men. There was very little literature, very little art, very little theology, and what was there was not exactly inspiring. It was all so insubstantial, people who found it as a fad felt free to make up what it meant as they went along.

Imagine my surprise when the culture decided to do this all over again. Witchcraft had another wave, this one aesthetically somewhere between Satanist goth and a potted plant. I clearly wasn't the only one looking for an exit ramp from American Christianity and religious culture, as an entire generation of women decided to declare themselves witches. But it wasn't as if all of the quiet, grounded covens suddenly swelled with members, or the intentional communities and societies found themselves inundated with new recruits. It was a generation of self-declared, singular witches, many of whom learned about witchcraft through Tumblr.

And other than praying to a goddess instead of Yahweh, and decorating themselves with elaborately colored hair rather than khakis, it was pretty much indistinguishable from Protestant-ism. Here they all were, praying for the fall of capitalism—you know, vaguely, and until that happens, can you please make sure I get a raise at work and draw more subscribers to my YouTube channel? Thanks, Hekate, goddess of the underworld, who probably has better things to do.

Every road we follow, hoping it will take us toward the future or revolution, takes us circling back to the past. There was a bit of a scandal on witch TikTok last year. The TikTok witches, it seems, decided to hex the moon. And the Twitter witches got upset, saying you can't hex the moon, there are consequences to that kind of impertinence. Some of the Twitter witches insisted they had, in their rituals, talked to Apollo, and now Apollo was pissed and wasn't going to do things for them. They didn't say what those things were, but it was probably along the lines of getting Justin Bieber tickets.

For some reason the whole thing sent me into a rage. "You did not talk to Apollo," I wanted to yell. Who do these girls think they are, lighting candles in an Ohio basement, thinking the god of poetry is going to take their call? Thinking they won't face madness or torment while trying to find the language of the divine? Thinking the saints who wandered in the desert for years begging god to speak to them must just not have used the right crystal? You don't get to talk to god and then just go to your job at the mall.

It's all so spiritually thin, this generation of witches making demands without devotion, looking to the stars to tell them when things will get good for them rather than asking what they can offer of themselves. At the end of the day, it's not so much witchcraft as enchanted capitalism—in other words, Protestantism.

My glimpse into the misogyny that made its way through the pagan communities was my first inkling that the problem with religion was not the text, it was the interpretation of that text. Men could totally agree that femininity is divine and then rape the women around them. And some Christians could read that only masculinity is divine and create wild, beautiful cults around the Virgin Mary, including writing and performing erotic plays about her life.

I wonder if one of the reasons we want religion to swarm into everything, to tell us what to do and eat, who we should love, what we should read, how we should behave, what our jobs should be, what to do with our bodies, is not about religious morality at all. It's about escape. And just choosing one thing, one system, one structure, one book, protects us from the terror of freedom. The terror of ourselves.

That self is going to fuck it all up, though. It's going to get in the way of whatever message we are so desperate to hear, the guidance we all need so much. One book was never going to be enough. Nor one reader.

I am not empty,
I am open

If we are to perish in the battles of the future, let us do our best to prepare ourselves to perish with a clear vision of the world we shall be leaving behind.

SIMONE WEIL

If this is how you treat your friends, no wonder you have so many enemies.

ST. TERESA OF AVILA, TO GOD

IF GOD IS DEAD, what are we going to do with his body?

They're going to tear down a church in Kansas City and build condos instead. Is that better or worse, I wonder, than the cathedral in Chicago, down the street from where I used to live, where the church itself was turned into condos. We, the outsiders, still got to wonder at the beautiful exterior, but now some rich asshole had a rose window in his living room.

Kansas City needs housing, but not housing like this. Not housing for the economically mobile, not housing with modern loftlike layouts and granite countertops and spacious interiors. It needs housing families can afford, not just stylish couples who work in advertising or pharmaceuticals or some other fucking soulless thing. It needs all the houses standing empty to be worth filling, it needs floors that aren't rotting and roofs that aren't leaking. Instead they keep building condos for these mythical happy white couples. Maybe they have a dog named after a fantasy television program they both enjoy.

There is another church near my house in Kansas City, and it takes up half a city block. On Sundays, I see only a handful of people coming and going. These are not the megachurches of the plains, packed with chinos and belted polo shirts, simply the cold, drafty stone foundations of devotion and solace. The way things look to be going, in the church and in the neighborhood and in the secular urban culture, it too will find itself shut down soon, and people will start plotting for what should take its place.

I imagine that when a developer looks at this building, they see lost profit. They see the structure transformed or replaced, filled with young professionals, maybe with a coworking space on the ground floor. I imagine that when a priest looks at the building, they see lost souls. They imagine it filled with the wayward sheep lost to a secular culture, the ghosts of the godless filling the pews. I imagine that when a community organizer looks at the building, they see a space for organizing. They see it filled with the work of local artists, or support groups for a very specific marginalized population.

When the check-cashing place two blocks from my house that had for years stood empty started to show signs of life, I thought, god, I hope they put some food in there. The only options for groceries in the neighborhood were a drugstore chain that had some chips and sodas, a gas station that had some chips and sodas, and a discount grocery store that had heavily processed canned and frozen foods and almost no fresh meat or vegetables. I started to dream of a greengrocer, or a New York–style bodega, despite the fact that a city where no one walks could never support such a place.

Or maybe it would be a decent place to eat. Foodie culture had taken over the city and wiped out most of the middle. It is a city of culinary extremes, like a lot of cities these days. Either you hit the fast-food places for fried chicken and burgers and chow mein and maybe a salad that is a pile of iceberg lettuce with two cherry tomatoes and one cucumber circle and a small plastic container of ranch dressing. Or you go high end, have a fifteen-dollar cocktail with gold leaf or rose petals or an orchid or a dried blood-orange wheel floating on top. Or a bologna sandwich that costs twenty dollars because it's artisanal hand-made bologna and artisanal homemade pimento cheese on artisanal homemade sourdough bread. Or a duck breast with blackberry sauce. Or a cheeseburger that costs fifteen dollars for reasons you can never actually figure out, that is not nearly as tasty as the five-dollar Winstead's double cheeseburger from the twenty-four-hour drive-through and is probably even worse for your body.

The specialization process, this relentless desire to make everything shiny and new and unexpected, just hollows out the middle. There are few places to get a beer and a decent meal for less than twenty dollars a person. There are few places to get anything simply made with care, rather than fussed over eternally or slapped together with maximum efficiency. You're either slumming or splurging. Even the barbecue places are branding themselves, jacking up prices so they can sell you a bottle of their secret sauce or a T-shirt. They invent special sandwiches, piling all kinds of garbage onto what should be an affordable puddle of sauced meat, and the people pay three dollars more for it, just to Instagram it with the geotags.

So when the windows got covered up and the sounds of hammering and maneuvering started to emerge, when cars showed up in the parking lot and people were seen moving in and out, I started to dream of a middle-class restaurant. It was too much to hope for the place I used to eat in Berlin when I was short on cash, with its pay-what-you-can scale—maintained strictly by the judgmental glowering of Germans who would stare pointedly at your fashionable shoes or nice jacket when you held out less than expected—where giant trays of good baked pastas or roasted meats, enormous bowls of salad and fruit, and stacks of bread were all laid out among bottles of terrible but drinkable red wine. Wouldn't that be a wonderful addition to the neighborhood, a place to go when it's 6:30 p.m., you're about to start making dinner, and you realize you forgot that you're totally out of onions and you're too tired to walk the mile and a half to the closest grocery store with a produce aisle.

What moved in instead was yet another arts nonprofit, handing out flyers for exhibitions and get-togethers. We have art, I thought. We have murals, we have galleries. The old bank that closed down a couple blocks away also got turned into a neighborhood gallery and arts space. We have outreach groups and a queer poetry circle that has barbecues and performances in the neighborhood park. There are bars that host open mic nights in the adjoining neighborhood. There are coffee shops all over Westport that show local artists' work. What we need is food. Or a clinic. Or childcare. Or a library with computers and the internet. We don't need more art. And we don't need more goddamn coffee. The swill at the gas station is usually better than the expensive stuff just north of the bus stop. Or down Troost. Or at that Starbucks with the fancy drive-through halfway between here and Westport. There's a lot of fucking coffee, is all I'm trying to say.

But of course people don't dream of adequately feeding someone, they don't go to med school in the hopes of providing basic care in exchange for a sustainable income. They dream of expansion, not maintenance. They dream of art, not groceries. They dream of leading a movement, not participating in one. They dream of the glorification of their own desires, not the meeting of other people's needs. Or they dream purely of profit, which means selling low quality in high quantity with little overhead, and of course treating employees decently and making sure they don't drop dead of a preventable disease counts as overhead.

Meanwhile the place across the street from the new arts nonprofit, which had been empty since I moved into the neighborhood a year ago and for god knows how long before that, put up a banner announcing it would soon open as a biscuit shop. The biscuits were artisanal and handmade. They started at six dollars each.

When I got together with my next-door neighbors, who love god and guns in that order, it was the neighborhood's livability we'd bitch about. How far we had to go to get a meal. How everyone had to learn to drive drunk really well because the bars were a couple neighborhoods over and it wasn't safe to walk home after dark. How far the grocery stores were. But everyone has a car, my neighbor would say, so maybe it doesn't matter. And yeah, everyone has a car as long as everyone you know has a good driving record and good credit and a steady enough income to handle any breakdowns. But I didn't have a car, because I couldn't afford one and I don't have a good driving record, so I'm on the ground here too. And on the ground means walking a mile and a half to the grocery store, before it gets too dark or too hot or too cold to be outside, then strapping your food to your body and carrying it back to your house. Or waiting for the bus, which also involves a lot of walking because there's not a direct route, and if you miss it by just a little, you'll be waiting more than half an hour for the next one.

Maybe I should be happy that those churches are mostly empty now. If someone abuses their authority, it is only right and good that their places should stand empty. And certainly, the churches abused their authority, shifting their attention from the divine to the biological: do this with your body, don't do that with your body. Ministers told parishioners that their poverty is a punishment from god for their sin, not the predictable product of a system of racism and exploitation. They told parishioners that if they fall pregnant from being raped, being coerced, being manipulated, or just from trying to stave off agonizing loneliness and emptiness, it is their duty to god to become mothers. They protected predators and did nothing to help either their victims or the offenders. They told parishioners there was only one life to lead, one text to study, one god to praise. They fell, and they deserved their fall.

But now we have all of their stuff lying around. We have the empty buildings. We have the Sunday mornings free. We have the charities and the infrastructure and the property. We have what is left from centuries of a dominant ideology and its supporting structures. So I repeat: if god is dead, what are we going to do with his body? Perhaps the best way to answer this question is to understand better the purpose it served in the first place.

There is still a certain type of atheist who can only think of god as delusion or as a malevolent force. If two peoples at war have different gods, it must be the belief in those gods that caused the wars. It can't be historic discrimination or lack of civil rights or oppression or any of the other things that come with majority/minority thinking. If someone who believes in a god did a bad thing, then eradicating that belief will prevent that bad thing from happening again. We definitely wouldn't just find another fucking reason to massacre, oppress, and eliminate one another.

It's the same thinking that leads to attempts at mass conversion. If we all believe in the same god, there won't be any problem. As if the god of Mexico City is the same as the god of Siberia or the god of Uganda. The no-god of Colombia will be similarly different from the no-god of Tulsa and the no-god of Szechuan.

But atheism is something else we can probably blame Martin Luther for. By stripping Christianity down from meaning to belief, he made it vulnerable to fact-checking. Thanks to Protestants' insistence that everything that isn't contemplative prayer, Bible reading, and belief in the story of Jesus Christ is paganism, all anyone really has to do to knock Christianity down is prove that Jesus did not exist, that the miracles were just tricks, or, if Christ did exist, that he didn't ascend bodily into heaven or didn't say the things the Bible claims he said, and so on. If you are told you are the only authority you need to interpret the Bible and decode its true meaning, why not also assume you are the only authority you need to decide whether God exists at all.

This must be why the atheists I met in Kansas were just as annoying as the Evangelicals I met in Kansas. No one was processing the trauma they experienced being raised under a monotheistic patriarchal religion very well, and the atheists rarely noticed that they hadn't actually escaped their upbringing but simply slid toward one end of the spectrum.

Belief is not interesting. One could say it is the crutch of children who need to believe life is magical, that Santa will visit them personally and grant their wishes, or that the pain and awkwardness of losing a tooth is ultimately profitable, but life is magical for children with or without candy-hiding bunnies. If anything, adults tell children to believe in these things to hide the true magic of the world from them. We tell them magic only exists in the realm of material goods, not that trees and rivers have spirits, that life is ruled by terrifying coincidence, that every single act we create can be layered with meaning.

If you tell me I have to go all-in on something having definitely happened, something unprovable for which the only documentation has been overtly and covertly doctored and manipulated and edited over many centuries, and then on top of all that I have to change my behavior and my nature and my desires, and if I don't I have to feel a lifetime of shame and disgust because I don't love in the right way or dress in the right way or pray in the right way, well, really, I'll think you're a fucking lunatic. Sure, pile it on, tell me the earth is only six thousand years old and every life on this earth is precious to God, because that is what basing a lifetime of decisions on belief does.

But if you tell me I should go all-in on faith, that I should change my behavior and my nature and my desires based on an essential faith that I can spend a lifetime creatively expressing, then sure, I'm there with you. That is what ritual is: an expression of faith, not belief. When I went to that witch and asked for a ritual for love, it wasn't out of a belief that it would work. It's easy to disprove magic. I did it out of faith that there was something not inherently disgusting and unforgivable about myself, and that that part of myself might be loved.

All the festivals are expressions of faith, not belief. Even if we're droning on about the baby Jesus and how miraculous it is that he was born to this virgin. Even if we're cynically winking at Joseph, implying that Mary was just trying to get out of trouble, magically explaining away a pregnancy—bitches be deceiving, am I right. The Christmas festival, though thoroughly corrupted by money and Santa, is ultimately about faith and not the belief in Jesus as our savior. The whole structure of it says, Here is our darkest season, and things can and will get rocky, and maybe that will last eternally and all of our stocks will be depleted, but we are going to show our faith, in the generosity of the divine and of the earth and of each other, by feasting just as winter begins.

Only Christianity and Islam truly rest their entire religions on questions of belief. Belief that these specific people truly existed and were truly blessed in this specific way. Everything is built around this tiny, incredibly unstable core. And the fact that the core is likely nonsense, and the furious nature of the defense when the nonsense is pointed out, only amplifies its instability. But that doesn't mean that everything built out of those religions was built on belief rather than faith, and it also doesn't mean that every single thing inspired by nonsense is inherently worthless.

And anyway, even if we believe Jesus was both a historical figure and a manifestation of divinity on earth, he was just another guy trying to bring about the end of the world. That's what much of his teachings point to, the end times he was trying to help bring about. And I'm just so tired of . . . etc. etc., you know how this goes by now.

Who is going to touch people now? That's what I keep wondering. If we get rid of nuns, I mean. Who is physically going to pick up and hold and bathe the sick, the poor, and the dying, if there are no more nuns?

Luther wanted to get rid of nuns. This probably had something to do with Katharina, a middle-aged nun who was inspired by Luther's writings, and who he helped smuggle out of her convent hidden in a fish barrel. They would later marry, and their own marriage became for Luther the ideal for all Protestant marriage. And don't we all decide that what works best for us is the way the whole world should be ordered. "Lord Katy," as he called her, was happy running her family like a business, managing all the household logistics while her husband thought things and said things out loud in front of crowds and wrote things down. And thus shall it be for all humankind.

Other women were "liberated" through the Reformation, liberated from the religious orders—and into what exactly? Into family life and sexuality. Katharina bore six children, two of whom died young. There was at least one miscarriage. Whether she enjoyed any of these sessions of impregnation is of course lost to time. She was, like all women, also liberated into capitalism. She turned the household into a generator of income, charging rent for Martin's students and acolytes, tending to livestock, brewing beer. The domestic sphere was entirely her responsibility, and she monetized every inch of it she could.

This is often seen as progress. Under the Protestant faith, women could, eventually, hold positions of power within the church. Women can be ministers, they say. Well, a woman still can't be god, so I'm not sure how progressive this truly is. But by taking away the cloister, the convent, and the veil, mostly what the Protestants did was board up the limited fire escapes out of secular culture, a culture of the horror of embodiment, the culture of predatory capitalism.

I'm not saying the Luthers invented the gig economy, but they certainly did not create a theology that would work against it. It's no wonder Protestantism, particularly as practiced in America, started to warp the relationship between god and capital. If there is no need for intermediaries, you don't need to find someone to petition god on your behalf, someone who might get your request not to starve to death wrong or send those heavenly rays of gold coins to the wrong supplicant. You can ask him yourself, and you can misinterpret obtaining that gold, or not, as a quantitative measure of god's love and desire for you not to starve to death.

Under Protestant capitalism, then, monetization simply gives god more opportunities to show you how much he loves you. So there is no reason not to turn everything in your life into a revenue stream. Your spare bedroom can be monetized so god can send you more love. Your children's lives can be documented and monetized in cute little YouTube videos so god can send you more love. Your hobbies can be monetized, your body can be monetized, your every thought can be monetized, all to bestow on you more of god's love. Any trouble you have with this arrangement only proves your unworthiness in god's eyes.

A generation younger than Katharina was St. Teresa of Avila. As Luther was working to shut down convents in Germany, Teresa was building more in Spain. Teresa warily watched him from a distance. The thing that finally pushed her into a convent after a long period of prayer and contemplation was her mother's death. Her mother had married at the age of fourteen, and she would give birth to ten children, with an unknown number of miscarriages, before she died less than twenty years later. Teresa was thirteen, only a year younger than her mother had been at her wedding. A long future—or more likely, a short one—of being pregnant, breastfeeding, getting pregnant, breastfeeding, getting pregnant, dying in childbirth lay ahead if she made the same decision.

The church was a way out of a short, sickly life of physically building a family out of her own body. That required the denial and denigration of that body through flogging and veiling. But it was a way out of production and toward something more like creation. The Catholic Church was an enormous machine of accumulation, of economic and cultural and political power, but it also provided pathways out of that mode for the individual. The abbey, the hospital, the beguinage, the convent, the cloister, the orphanage, and the monastery weren't just providers of services. They were islands in the sea of capital.

The rise of Protestantism, then, was a rise in the water level, and firm ground started to disappear under people's feet. Now, in the Midwest, maybe if you stand on tiptoe you can get your nose and mouth above the waterline, but otherwise you are immersed in secular, capitalist culture. If you are an artist, you are an artist for the market and not for the glory of god. If you are a scholar, you are a scholar in the academic marketplace and not for the glory of god. If you are a doctor, you are a doctor for the American health care system and not for the glory of god. But the sad thing is how easily people confuse the two.

And if you are a woman, you are a woman for the nuclear family and not for the glory of god. Being a woman still has one exit possible, into marriage with a wealthy partner. You can get out of the marketplace through your husband's strong position within the marketplace. But wealthy marriages are their own kinds of industry.

Let the drunk, angry ghost of Christopher Hitchens rail on about all of the abuses that happened on those little islands. Not everyone who was a nun wanted to be a nun. There was physical, spiritual, emotional abuse, rape, genocide. There was exploitation and silencing. All of these things have been used as an argument for eradicating these spaces, but without any understanding or care about the good they did.

There was also physical, spiritual, emotional abuse, rape, genocide out in the secular culture. There was exploitation and silencing. Colonialism and war. Bigotry and misogyny. Terrorism and hatred. There's nowhere to go that isn't that.

Charity is not an adequate replacement. A communal garden, kitchen, and shared meals are not easily replaced by a food pantry. A neighborhood with friendship and care and support is not easily replaced by a shelter. A careworker is not easily replaced by a caseworker. A calling is not easily replaced by a job. If you're drowning in that water, the most you can hope for is a snorkel, or maybe an inflatable raft if you're living during a time of leftist resurgence, but an entire little stable world, not a chance.

It's not just the material support, it's the ability to think and live and breathe outside of market forces and secular culture. To be unreachable, untouched. Not just to work against the marketplace but not to acknowledge its existence at all.

I think about Catherine of Siena drinking pus to force herself to get over her disgust with a dying body. As a nun, she tended to the sick and, faced with active decay and leaking fluids, felt a natural revulsion. She knew the limitation disgust put on her ability to care for these bodies, not only to be in contact with them but to ease the mind of the person suffering, who needs the care tremendously but is also ashamed of their smell, their appearance, their physical condition.

It is terrible to be a body. You can contain the horror by maintaining your body on your own, figuring out how to nourish and protect it. To keep it in fine form and pleasing to the eye. To care for all of its odder needs behind closed doors, such that its more extreme sounds and excretions and smells are witnessed only by you. When it exceeds those boundaries and becomes other people's problem, you can only pray the person who comes to help won't make that face that lets you know what your body is doing to them.

I once joked with a friend that if I ever kept a pregnancy, I would crawl into a closet and give birth by myself like a cat. Her job would be to guard the door and never let anyone ever see me in that state, but also to stay close in case medical intervention became necessary. It is not just the shitting myself or the vaginal display, but the idea of someone witnessing my pain and my inability to keep everything under control that I found unbearable. My friend agreed. "When it's all over, I'll make you a martini."

Probably Catherine went too far with the pus thing, but nuns always put their hands on people whose bodies were seen not only as disgusting but as dangerous. They touched lepers. They touched people with AIDS when people were still freaking out about letting gay people use water fountains.

Meanwhile, there have been feminists arguing online for years now that if you want their time and attention, as a friend, you should Venmo them. Deeply distorting the term emotional labor, they insist all of their time can be considered billable hours, and if you need something from them, you had better expect an invoice. Having lived in the waters of secular culture for so long, they can't even dream anymore of dry land; they insist that any effort they put in, any deed for which they are not well compensated, is essentially exploitation. It's labor to text you back when you're having a panic attack; you're taking advantage, asking me to read your manuscript without offering to pay me; it's abuse to tell me your problems without first asking about mine.

And sure, they'll touch your disgusting body, and maybe they won't even wrinkle their noses when they do it, but they'll do it because they are paid to do it. Because why else should they? Just hire someone. If you can't afford it, get your family to do it, that's what they are for. And if they won't do it because you are gay, because your family is full of assholes, because they're dead, well, just please try to die out of sight without bothering too many people about it.

That tight interconnectedness is a form of control, of course. The reason it is so difficult to leave traditional communities, even when they become abusive, is that stepping outside of that sphere is like stepping into the fucking jungle where you can already see the tiger ready to pounce.

I used to worry, as a child, that I would end up in some sort of apocalyptic death cult. The Jonestown massacre happened just a few months after I was born, and I was allowed to watch the HBO movie about the incident at a much too early age. Since then it has been an object of real fascination and fear. The fear comes because when I listen to the early sermons of Jim Jones, all gloriously archived on the internet, I have a hard time disagreeing with anything he says.

Why, if Jesus taught us to embrace poverty and simplicity, are there preachers driving around in Cadillacs? Why, if Jesus taught us to love our neighbor, is there segregation in the churches? Why, if Jesus hung out with the Marys, is there so much hatred of women in Christianity?

Jim Jones must have felt like shelter. To have built a community, free of these forms of discrimination, free from the pressures of secular life, free from the political and societal insanity of the 1970s—I might have run to sign up. Well, except that the music was terrible, and there was no art, and the food in the commune sounds pretty bad. I might have lasted twenty-four hours before I started scheming to get my passport back.

Because where else are you going to find refuge from secular society these days except in an apocalyptic death cult? These days, even monasteries have to manage tourists and offer spiritual retreats to white women who say namaste in the chapel in order to stay afloat. The money to pay off all those kids whose lives they ruined has to come from somewhere.

I don't think a bunch of teenagers across Europe and the US fled to join ISIS because they had studied sharia law and determined that would be the most logical way of organizing society and managing behavior. I think they looked at our consumerist culture, at the expectation we'll fall into ecstatic states when the latest Baby Yoda product is revealed, and thought, I have a gnawing emptiness and a deep need for meaning, and waiting for a streaming service that caters directly to my needs isn't going to fulfill me. Or they looked at their options for hedonistic abandon and realized that depravity quickly gets boring. Or they couldn't stand the cognitive dissonance of political hypocrisy and the lived experience of oppression and marginalization any longer. Or they had violent urges and ISIS would let them shoot people. I just don't think it had anything to do with god.

How does one find meaning in a land filled with shopping malls, online pornography, cheery Facebook status updates, a looming police presence, five superhero movie events a year, disposable friendships, plastic bags stuck in trees, false eyelashes, memes that superimpose philosophical quandaries over cartoon imagery, hot Cheetos, very important opinions about craft beers, parking lots, credit scores, Instagram face-tuning, a three-hour wait to see the Mona Lisa, prescription medication, sexy vampires, boy bands, factory farming, photos of drowned children washing up on the shore, Nazi YouTubers, limited-edition sneakers, contouring, bingeable television, faux fur, bathroom breaks that are monitored by your employer, advice columns, debt, bikini bodies, astrology podcasts, neighborhood watch, mass-transit fare hikes, forever wars, restaurant delivery services, influencers, celebrity DJs, paying to watch other people play video games, talk shows, your father chuckling at a mild-mannered joke made by an NPR host, disappointing series finales, landfills, true crime, teenagers thirsting for dead serial killers, CBD ice cream, lip filler, climate-change deniers working for the *New York Times*, candy-colored plastic vibrators, sea turtles killed by plastic straws, carcinogens in our breast tissue, hot takes, *Sex and the City* DVD box sets, political debates about who is allowed in which bathroom, a suicide epidemic, ten-thousand-dollar health insurance deductibles, Crocs, nootropics, mushroom coffee and creatine, middle-aged women lusting after Timothee Chalamet, Oscar winner Emma Stone, the Iowa Writers Workshop, CIA-led assassinations and coups, bubble tea, "daddy," stan culture, Gamergate, purple Skittles, Superfund sites, intermittent fasting, paycheck loans, Carl Andre's acquittal in the mysterious death of Ana Mendieta, Sea-World, cognitive behavioral therapy and SSRIs, luxury cheeseburgers coated in gold leaf, and real housewives.

How does one create a sense of both self and divinity in a world that assesses your worth based on an algorithm? That forces you to commodify and data-fy your apartment, your brand, your hobbies, your relationship, your social media presence, your opinions about television shows, your car, your play time, your fitness routine, your driving habits, your grocery store purchases, your reading habits, your online shopping. Not only to survive under late capitalism but to keep up with your peers in the constant performance of your identity?

It is possible to find meaning, peace, divinity, and self in this culture, but it's a tough climb to get there. We make it tougher by the day. It's easy to imagine someone on the cusp of stepping into all of that deciding, fuck it, a caliphate sounds better. Or a suicide cult. Or a commune in South America that requires you to sign over all of your possessions to join. At least then maybe you can just read a book without formulating the six-hundred-word review you'll be paid twenty-five dollars for, or write a song without having to upload it to a streaming service, or read the news without having to formulate an opinion. Or not read the news at all, because what good does it do you, sitting in Topeka, Kansas, to know the ins and outs of the war in Syria, and which side you agree with?

Tell me the way out of this terrible world. Other than marrying some rich guy and living in the Catskills (while keeping a tasteful apartment in Manhattan for entertaining, of course). Show me any other way of being, any other way of feeling, any other way of experiencing life. Because this world will grind any divine spark out of you unless you fight hard to protect it.

We got rid of the convents, we set the Waco compound on fire, hell, we even got mostly rid of ISIS. Where is a painfully sensitive teenager to go to find refuge and meaning?

Once people have steady ground under their feet, they can start to look up. Not just down at the ground, where they have to double-check for hidden crevasses or unstable stones, but to look ahead and above.

And one way of creating that steady ground is through cash. When a person's path was purposefully destabilized by fraud, by systematic oppression, by abuse, by violence, by manipulation, it is only right that their path be stabilized by the institution that caused the problems. Let he who created the obstacles not only remove those obstacles but help make up the lost ground. So here's some money. Churches give big payouts to the children their personnel interfered with sexually. Governments give big payouts—or talk about it endlessly without ever doing it—to those they enslaved or tried to murder, or the children of those they enslaved or murdered.

Money is good. It pays for things like therapy and education, it relieves pressure, it gives a person the opportunity to look ahead and above. But it also enables. It provides new opportunities to self-harm or zone out with opioids or booze. Money is only healing if the person receiving it is ready to be healed. If they still want to get fucked up or self-destruct, money will facilitate those processes as well.

Giving money is often a way of relieving oneself of responsibility. Here, take it, fuck up the rest of your life for all I care. Now I sound like one of those people who insist they won't give money to someone asking for it on the street because they'll just waste it on drugs. If you're living on the street, you could probably use some drugs. The two dollars you deign to give, with a turned head and a small sneer, isn't going to pay for a motel room or a security deposit or a decent interview outfit or long-term therapy to address long-term abuses and trauma. Go get fucked up man, it's on me.

Obviously the best thing to do would be to create a non-hellish environment for people who are in need, and money is not the way to do that. Hells are as internal as they are external, and the solution can't be to drug people, put them in a broken mental health system (or jail), and hope the containment of their bodies and neurotransmitters will shore them up. People whose lives are shattered deserve a team willing to take the time to get out the glue and gather the pieces and assist in putting them back together in a form that makes sense for everyone.

But the way we give money, as a way of absolving ourselves—as if it's the only thing we need to do rather than the first thing we need to do—only creates more problems. For all the money we give to charity, we should have a world where no one goes hungry, everyone has access to clean water, all villages have adequate schools. But charity distorts, it is taken advantage of, and it creates relationships that are easy to manipulate.

Wouldn't it be better, then, if we used the assets of the church, the assets currently just lying around, to stabilize what is needed in the lives of those it destabilized? For all the queers excommunicated, shelter. For women whose bodies were degraded and used through forced motherhood, care and rest. For those who were raped, groped, and assaulted, relief and support. And they should also be given cash.

I detest waste. Every time I throw a moldy bag of grapes or a withered carrot into the trash, I feel like I have failed. If I had only organized my menu or my day or my grocery shopping a little better, I could have incorporated those grapes and that carrot into my body. If I find a sweater I had forgotten I owned that has been languishing in the back of my closet for years, I regret not having incorporated it into my outfit rotation. Every time I move houses, and I move a lot, I look at the two tablespoons of ground cinnamon left in the bottom of the jar and wonder, "Who could use this? Who can I give this to?" No one ever wants it.

I don't really worry about wasted money. Money is an abstraction now. We just print it, create it on a computer screen, turn it into ones and zeroes. And yet we still withhold it from people who could turn it into something that exists in the real world. When I fling money off, I feel no real connection to its destination or purpose; it's an entirely fake thing that sometimes I have and often I do not.

But I worry about all other wasted resources. I want us to gather and distribute. And the human resources I worry most about squandering are the resources of love and care. Not only that which we squander on men who don't text back or forget to tell us they are married or women who . . . whatever, everyone is terrible and behaves terribly. I worry about the love and care that gets lost inside of people who are trapped in their own traumas. Those who have to watch their feet to ensure they don't end up back on their asses. Everything they have to give and we reject as a society because they don't or can't express it in the way we want them to.

The way to tap those resources is to help them stabilize. That's what the church did, if only for some. We can gather those resources that still exist and distribute them. It's all still there.

Help me make the most of freedom and of pleasure

I FIRST STARTED TALKING to the Virgin Mary when a man I knew went missing overseas. He had been gone for months, with no updates. All anybody knew was that the ransom he was being held for was astronomical, rescue was unlikely, and he could be missing from our lives for a very long time.

It was hard to do things like get up and walk around, put on clothes, go to work, talk to people. It's acute for the first week or so, this never-ending pain in your chest, the leaky faucet of your face. But as the days go on and it becomes clear that you are going to have to continue to live your life while you wait, you learn to compartmentalize. You learn to function, and that functioning feels like a betrayal. Because this person is gone, and the whole world should be made to feel the ache of that. The absence should be catastrophic.

We were not lovers, not yet. When we met we were both in relationships, and we circled one another. I would have to grip the Formica counter when he was around to keep from jumping on top of him, but I was respectful. We talked about it. We were both going to go away for work, and when we came back we would see. Only he did not come back, and I was being crushed under this enormous and weighty dot dot dot.

At the time, a lot of people—journalists, aid workers, soldiers, contractors, the unlucky, the brave, the better than us—were being taken overseas and videos were being made and broadcasted of their deaths. It wasn't something you had to picture, horrifically, in the privacy of your brain. You and millions of others got to see the person you love, with their long, lovely hands and their eyes and the way they tried to keep themselves from laughing until their controlled smile exploded as their whole face opened up, have their head cut off.

So functioning wasn't happening at any sort of high level. We were making do. For me, I would not think about it, which was an active process and frankly exhausting, except sometimes I would notice I was thinking about it. Like when I was in his neighborhood, which was my neighborhood, because he lived just a couple streets over, and I would notice I was looking for him in the crowd. Just minding my own business, trying to get to the grocery store, and I'd be looking up for the top half of his face, he was so unusually tall, like something one would decide to climb as a challenge. I would notice myself doing this, I would remember bumping into him, and the rest of the day was destroyed.

But I got better at the functioning, and I found two outlets for thinking about him. One was when I'd get drunk and search his name to see if a video of his execution had been released. When I found nothing, I would cry until I fell asleep. The other was on my knees in front of the Virgin Mary in any cathedral I could find. I would light a candle, I would pray for the Virgin to make her presence known to him and provide even a glimmer of comfort, and I would choke out the sobs that I had been stockpiling in my body during the previous weeks of functioning.

Why the Virgin Mary? Why not Saint Anthony, the patron saint of the missing? Why not Saint Patrick, the patron saint of the kidnapped and enslaved? Why not Saint Christopher, the patron saint of travelers who are stupid and insist on being in places they don't belong and go into territories where people are abducted all the time and should frankly know better and listen to all of the people saying, this is dumb, don't do this?

Maybe it's that I can't imagine praying about a missing man to the same saint I'm supposed to bug about a missing sock. And maybe it's that I preferred to talk to someone who knew what it was like to lose a man they loved and cared for. Hers was only gone for three days, but what a three days that must have been. Jesus descended into hell, but so did Mary.

I also prayed to Penelope, and any other archetype I thought might understand what I was going through. Because no one on earth did. Where in the twenty-first century was I going to find a support group for people whose loved ones had been kidnapped by pirates? Where was I going to find the solace of commiseration and shared experience? Where was I going to find someone with whom I could talk about what I was going through who wasn't immediately going to say, "I'm sorry, what?" or laugh or make me explain the whole story and then make jokes about what a great movie this was going to make when he was released. Only in the Virgin's presence could I find solace. Only in the stories of Penelope leading other men on and distracting herself with random hobbies could I find an accurate representation of my life.

It made me wonder what was going on in everyone else's life that we keep seeing the Virgin Mary. When it comes to great Christian sightings, nothing draws a crowd like a sighting of the Virgin Mary, in the clouds, in the water stain under the bridge, against a gable wall, in dreams, in a hospital, under a tree, in a tortilla. It's easy to make jokes about people being so delusional and so intellectually eroded by religious dogma that they will literally worship a tortilla, but to me it says nothing other than that people keep showing our enormous need.

If you are Christian and take the Marian apparitions as legitimate, it should make you wonder what is going on in heaven that it's Mary who keeps showing up back on earth. Does God know what she's up to? What is Jesus doing that he's too busy to make personal visitations, or is he aware that everyone is so ramped up for the end of the world that the moment he shows his face someone will launch an arsenal of nuclear warheads? Do they send her out as a messenger, or is she sneaking out when no one is looking?

You also have to wonder about Mary's motivations. She's been downgraded and written off by the church, she's been lied about and turned into a soft and mushy mom figure by so many of her believers. She had her life derailed by her god, her son, her state, and still she comes for us. She reappears to heal us, to comfort us, to talk with us. Is she really just so bored up in heaven, or is this what love is actually supposed to be?

If you don't believe in Christianity, the questions are still plenty provocative. Why is it this woman, not even an official goddess although worshipped for centuries as one, the one people need to see so badly they conjure her out of nothing? What makes her the subject of our collective hallucination, and not the son of God, or God himself? Why do we need her so much that we keep creating her?

We've always needed her. The church has always insisted she's not a goddess, and we have always insisted on worshipping her as one. The church kept trying to bend us back to the boys, saying, okay, yeah, she's great and we'll make her queen of the heavens or whatever, but she's not, like, *divine* or anything. And still people set up shrines, they set up festivals and lay services, and still people centered their worlds around her to the point of seeing her in a cup of coffee. The artists of the church, perhaps sick of painting one broken male body after another, kept putting her at the center of their paintings, where she opens up her robes to reveal all of the world's sinners housed there, like a broody hen sitting on orphaned kittens. It's not technically her job, but she'll do it because it has to be done.

On one hand, I believe that patriarchal monotheistic religion has caused profound psychological and spiritual damage to its followers, no matter which of the religions we're contemplating. On the other, I don't think people are stupid, or addicted to dogma, or incapable of compensating for the inadequacies of ideological systems with things like Marian worship. I also don't think the solution is to say, what if we understood God to be genderless? because there's too much history and theology and too many painful schisms to walk back with a new pronoun now. I also don't think there's a direct corollary between goddess worship and egalitarian treatment on earth. If we suddenly created a new religion that was either genderless or had gods and goddesses and nonbinary figures of divinity with an equal distribution of labor, that wouldn't create peace on earth. But still, the lack, the Mary-shaped hole, it consumes that which is around it.

I had to seek Mary out, she was not a part of my religious upbringing. The story of her birthing Christ, sure, but she was a vessel, a human, nothing more. There was no glorious Virgin figure in our church, no place to light a candle and sob. I don't remember her even coming up in sermons except around Christmas, usually coupled with messages about how women should just do what God tells them, which is to give birth. (Although I do remember one Sunday school discussion: "What if Mary had been able to abort Jesus? Abortion clinics could have left us all . . ." well, as Jews, I guess is what he was saying, but did it never occur to him that God could simply try again with another woman? Christ, the lack of imagination in these people.)

I wonder if it matters that by the time I found her I did not believe in the resurrection of Christ our Lord and Savior. If there was a historical Jesus, he was probably just a man who believed the world was about to end, thought that was going to be a good thing, and wanted everyone to get ready for it. So if I don't believe in a divine Jesus, nor in a patriarchal god, nor in the story of the virgin birth, what was I doing on my knees in front of Mary?

How in this age of skepticism and scientific realism and rational thought can we find a place for our spiritual longings without being an asshole about it? How does one avoid being a white girl in an ashram, saying things like god is god, decorating her apartment with one Shiva, one Buddha, one Mary—"you can just take what you need from each tradition and discard the rest, it's fine." Wearing a red Kabbalah string on one wrist with a Tantric tattoo on the other. Or a basement-dwelling weirdo, worshipping an Egyptian snake goddess they know nothing about, or one specific tree, "because all that really matters is the ritual."

Meanwhile, the news is full of men who call themselves gurus and use the spiritual hunger of others to rub their crotches on people. Twist your body this way and you'll find enlightenment, no, not like that, here let me help you, it's there in your pelvis, let me, ahhh. A lot of people who, because they felt good and peaceful in someone's presence, thought they must be spiritually evolved rather than just having a nice Neptune placement in their charts, and they worshipped that person like an Egyptian snake goddess.

Spirituality is a T-shirt in our culture, something to buy and put on and take off whenever you want. Religion is brand loyalty, a devotion to an institution that doesn't actually care about you, and your only job, really, is to buy whatever new release it decides to put out and defend it rabidly online. Our consumerist identity has swallowed up our every need and impulse. We are all just looking for the newest, best, most highly rated product to add to our homes and fix our lives. And yes, I have a Virgin Mary in my home, thank you for asking. I also have a St. Teresa and a St. Therese. I have a print of Kali from a trip to Calcutta and some Islamic calligraphy. I have a saint candle with Jesus on it, and I have a saint candle with Courtney Love. I have a skull from the Day of the Dead that a friend gave me after another friend killed himself. I have crystals and minerals that were gifted by the spiritual and the superstitious, and a few I bought myself because they look nice. I have remnants of the love spell the witch did for me.. I have peacock feathers to represent the goddess Juno, and I have a lot of books on Greek gods and goddesses, many of which define the divine beings as psychological archetypes, not figures worth building temples to.

I went to Bali to write about digital nomads, Americans and Brits sequestering themselves in cheap, far-off places they interact with very little and understand even less to design apps and live the good life. On a day with nothing much to do I went to a temple. There was a sign at the entrance: if you are a menstruating woman, do not enter to avoid defiling the place. I was not menstruating, I entered, and then I wondered if my presence supported a place that discriminated against women, even if that "place" is an ancient religion.

But maybe it's good? Maybe one should have rituals about things like menstruation, things that are experienced as complicated and painful and confusing for a lot of people, in order to put them into some lineage and some larger context. Even if they are experienced as oppression, even if they have helped establish taboos against things that are natural, maybe they can be changed to be methods of empowerment. Rituals are helpful, and maybe weapons can be repurposed as tools. When I got back to my rented room, I started googling "menstruation rituals + new" to see if young feminists were perhaps reclaiming these rites on their own terms.

But then maybe it's just uniformly bad? How many women are allowed to consciously reform rituals for their own use, rather than being forced to participate in them without conscious reappropriation? Does the entire existence of the ritual separate men from women, creating the opportunity for difference of reality to be transformed into difference of quality? Does acknowledgment of difference always create a hierarchy? But then, does pretending difference does not exist do the same? Saying men and women are the same can create the idea that men and women should be the same, with men being the default, creating new layers of shame for anything that does not adhere to masculine stereotypes, right? And anything that is the basis for shame can be twisted into a form of superiority given the opportunity.

I remember being a teenager, reading third-wave feminists and listening to Ani DiFranco sing songs about periods. Menstruation is a gift, it is a power, it is proof that only women can bring life into this world. Before then, we had centuries of being told menstruation was disgusting, something to be hidden and ashamed of, something to suffer. We had doctors telling us this, we had our mothers telling us this, we had God telling us this. (Some gods. The Methodist god seemed to have nothing to say on the subject; it never came up.) So of course women wanted to reclaim it and say, actually, menstruation is great. And I read those feminist zines, which told me to use a diva cup or free-bleed and not be ashamed, and I listened to "Blood in the Boardroom": "These businessmen got the money / they've got the instruments of death / But I can make life / I can make breath." I read Jewish women reclaiming the mikveh ritual post-menstruation bathing, claiming they found it an empowering reminder of their life-giving forces.

Then a couple decades later I read a lot of the same kinds of women discriminating against trans women. What they had used to prop up their own feelings of disempowerment they now used to disempower others. I read Ani DiFranco defend a folk festival that chose to ban trans women from attendance, because their biological reality did not align with "real" women. I read feminists who worship Earth Mothers and Moon Goddesses say that women who didn't have children aren't real women, and this seemed to include infertile women. I read the same Jewish women who championed the mikveh say they couldn't accommodate trans men who menstruated. If they invested a lot of spiritual and psychological meaning into being menstruating people, people who couldn't menstruate because they couldn't biologically do so must be somewhere in the category of "other."

I was thinking about all of this while standing in a sacred space. I couldn't just bow, or fall into a trance, or pay a tribute and ask for a prayer and go on my little way. My head wouldn't stop spinning. What do we do with the place where the real world intersects with the spiritual world? I dealt with the issue by adding a print of a Bali mythological hag to my collection.

Once you reject the religion of your upbringing, any search

for a replacement starts to look like cultural appropriation. Any seeking feels like shopping. Once you lose your credulity, it begins to feel impossible to get it back, unless you willingly relinquish it to any wacko who promises you easy answers. There are a lot of religion's lost children—the feminists, the queers, the hungry, the sinners, the fuck-ups, the abused— standing outside the church doors wondering what the fuck to do now.

It's easy to say, worship what is divine and reject what is man-made, but there is no clear separation between the two. And anything divine needs a man-made machine to act as interpreter and filter. There's a reason why there are stories in every tradition about someone coming in contact with the divine and going mad or catching fire or whatever. What's the difference between a vision and a hallucination? Surely we're not going to let the person afflicted with one or both try to figure that out. And surely we're not going to allow other fields to take over here, just let science say everything is a hallucination, everything is neurochemistry or evolutionary psychology or whatever bullshit they come up with to explain things like God now.

When I started to feel the feelings about the Virgin Mary, I coped the way I always do. I did some research. I read theological discussions about the role of the Virgin Mary, including about a hundred pages of debate about the status of the Virgin Mary's hymen. (Was it restored by God? Did the angels remove Christ through Mary's side, leaving her vagina intact? Etc.) I read accounts of healings, both by those who were healed and by those whose official job it was to determine whether those healings were legitimate miracles. I read accounts of visions, both by those who beheld and by those whose official job it was to determine whether those visions were legitimate miracles.

I read psychological interpretations of the archetype of the virginal mother, and whether a clear line could be made from Mary to Artemis. I looked at artistic renderings of Mary, everything from "we don't actually know where the breast is" medieval art to the Pietà to folk art. I listened to a thousand versions of *Ave Maria*, by both classically trained musicians and pop stars. I read histories of the church, feminist criticisms of the church, queer studies about the church. I read the apocryphal gospels and studies of what was left out of the Bible. I read testimony from the Inquisition about people's prayers to Mary, read spells from various peasant populations that blended prayers with magic.

And look, I wish I could tell you I figured it out. I wish I could say, no, it's the authority of the church we have to listen to, they obviously got it right. Mary is a lady, a special one, and we should follow church doctrine on how we approach her. I equally wish I could say, actually, it's the people's version of Mary that makes sense, we should follow their lead when it comes to her elevation and our devotion. But I can't say either. A lot of people have fucked-up ideas of how a woman and a mother should be, is what I guess I am saying.

We're terrible at managing variety. It's not the authorities who balk at anyone trying to recreate or reimagine what they consider already established. Authorities like their authority and will incorporate the most powerful ideas from below as a way of neutralizing them. The idea of a Mary who contains the world—making her, not god, the highest deity—came out of Marian cults and a lot of medieval artwork, but the church found ways of absorbing this imagery, both to show its followers that it was adaptable and keep them from leaving, and to remove the potency of the idea and image. What it acknowledged, it could control. Authority is slow to acknowledge variety, but it must do so eventually, or the authority will fail and another will take its place.

True intolerance for variety comes instead from individuals. If you believe Mary gave birth through her side rather than having her hymen restored after a vaginal birth, well, you are absolutely insane, what is even wrong with you. There is too much in this world to believe in or disbelieve in. One way of protecting ourselves from having to constantly hear other perspectives, judge their worthiness, and adapt our beliefs as a result of new information is to believe instead in purity. Certainty. This is the only truth, I've figured it out, and you are a fool or a heretic or a devil in disguise if you don't bow down and share my certainty.

There is the divine, which is unknowable, a big mystery. Then there is our way of trying to know it. Human brains can't contain so much, can't work with mystery. Even mathematicians like Georg Cantor who tried to work with the concept of infinity had to go off to the asylum for a while. So we use metaphor and image—or we did before the Protestant Reformation turned religion into a list of things to do and not do. But still, we use metaphor and image, and the metaphor and images that will be the most useful to each of us come out of some kind of psychological complex, because they absolutely have to. So what is useful and meaningful to one person will depend on their relationship to their mother, which kindergarten teacher they had, what they first accidentally got an erection seeing, these kinds of things. That the metaphors and images are individual and psychologically based, rather than abstract and universal, does not make them less powerful. In fact, it makes them more powerful.

The problem becomes that most people don't know their psychological realities. They are totally unaware how fucked up their relationship with their mother is, they have to get wasted before they half-feel how disappointing their father was, they think their sexuality is normal and not an enormous fucking problem like it is for everyone else. Because they don't know their psychological selves, and there's so little in our culture that will foster such awareness—even therapy is now about how to be a well-functioning cog in the capitalistic machine and not how to navigate one's own psyche—they cling to rigid notions of purity. They will want to see a world that reflects only their inner selves because they otherwise have no idea what that inner self looks like. And maybe that's not so bad if you're sitting alone in your room, but if you're a leader of something or if you happen to find a lot of other people who believe in the same kind of purity, suddenly you're releasing sarin gas in a subway system, trying to bring about the end of the world, the ultimate form of purity.

I've always liked the gnostic idea that everyone is a priest. I found gnosticism through queer culture. A bunch of people shut out of institutional religion went looking for a tradition that would accept them and help them flourish, and there was gnosticism. There's no church, no hierarchy, no emphasis on biological behaviors like regulating sexuality or enforcing the sacred nature of the nuclear family that had rejected and tried to destroy them. There are no lifelong priests whose job is to condemn and scold and abuse their powerful position. But gnosticism still recognizes the need for the occasional intervention, for a filter and a reality check between us and god. The need that all of us have to voice our darkest, dumbest thoughts and hear back in return from someone who knows, "Yeah, what are you even talking about?"

It feels useful to me to have a religion that has no known origin. No one knows where gnosticism came from exactly—

there is no one document, no one prophet or story. This entirely removes the tradition from "belief" and makes it solely about faith. I also find it useful to have a religion that has survived for centuries without an infrastructure or institutional control. People still fall into gnosticism despite the lack of missionaries, despite the lack of sidewalk preachers, despite the lack of buildings and structures and leaders. Denounced as heretics by the Christian establishment throughout time, gnostics shrug and get on with it. Gnosticism waits for you, like a secret, and you find it when you need it.

With gnosticism, absent the hierarchy of the established church and the priests and cardinals and pope issuing doctrinal ideology from afar, your religion is both your problem and your responsibility. But who has that kind of time, I wonder. I like the idea of religion as a problem, because of the implication that it is never going to be solved. It will always be a Rubik's cube, and you will always be the idiot who can't work in algorithm, spinning colored squares and trying futilely to make them all line up. If we make that clear at the beginning, maybe people won't look for one easy thing to swallow and be done with. Religion can be something we endlessly fidget with at the back of our minds.

And it can allow everything that isn't essential to go away. Like stuff about Mary's hymen. We can all acknowledge that we don't actually need to know that, or the exact process of transubstantiation and all of the other stuff that falls under "belief" rather than "faith." Not that I don't love that stuff, but if it could be slated as a collection of thought experiments or wild speculation—imaginative flourishes rather than a hardline truth—it might save us all a lot of time.

When we are all priests, we can understand that not everything someone says is going to be interesting. We can question their authority. We can get used to questioning authority. And to having our own authority questioned. I would like to believe that everyone being a priest means they would take the role seriously, although I know too many dickbags to actually believe it. There'll always be someone playing devil's advocate, someone trolling, someone trying to spoil the sincerity of the people around them. They'll be up there, pretending like they're going to say something meaningful, then they'll start quoting "What if God Was One of Us" lyrics and trying to humiliate those for whom this is a serious business. And it'll be our job to recognize that this person is a priest too. That to tolerate the troll is to lighten our seriousness. And if a troll can't develop into someone capable of taking other things seriously, well, you know, they're probably a Gemini, it's not really their fault.

But who has this kind of time? The time to know and directly experience god, it's exhausting. Back when I lived alone, in a house that felt like a cave, when I had no intermediary between myself and my endless thoughts, I thought maybe I could know god. I had nothing but time to pray and study and be at their feet. It was excruciating. Now I'll throw anything between my thoughts and me, any silly distraction or other person or book, just to avoid feeling the pull of the unknown. I'll throw in Twitter, I'll throw in an entire husband, I'll throw in self-taught embroidery and a Henry James novel and eighty bottles of champagne. The material world is hard enough to stick with, the heavens are just a big distraction.

The years spent in pursuit, however, did something surprising. I always thought, once I got out of my rebellious, idiotic atheist phase, that pursuing god would unleash me from earth. That it would make me more suicidal, that it would untie whatever loose bonds I had managed to form. Maybe I chased god because I wanted an excuse not to be on the planet, but I found the chase did the opposite. It made me love the earth. It made me want to participate in the world.

If the divine is perfection and the earth is imperfection, why would one want to associate oneself with the earth? Why mess with the broken and the painful? It felt true, this gnostic idea that the broken world could only have been created by a broken deity. Yahweh is a bully and a creep, a puffed-up narcissist who woke up one day next to a kingdom and assumed it was a reflection of his own glory. Part of the pursuit of god, then, must be to find what is hidden behind that. Who is there in heaven other than these diminished little thunder gods?

For many gnostics, because the world was created by a debased deity, a lower form of divinity, we must reject his gifts. The body is a nightmare, the world a horror show. The best thing to do is turn away from it all, protect oneself, wait for this world to burn and this body to die and be off to the next thing. To pursue the world is to pursue only loneliness and despair, brokenness and the irredeemable.

But admitting brokenness is surely the first step toward repair. Admitting a broken connection between what is human and what is truly divine is the first step toward establishing new lines of communication. And if our bodies are profane, then there is no need for purity or disembodiment. It's not even possible. So why not explore the pleasures it can bring. If there is no such thing as sin, only folly, what possibilities for engagement does that open up?

In gnosticism, the story of the fall of Adam and Eve finds new meaning. It is Sophia, divine wisdom, that offers knowledge and not the devil, and the reception of this knowledge is not a betrayal but instead a kind of pact. Tossing the humans out of the garden and into a barren material existence is an act of love.

Here, go learn some things. Go get fucked up. Make mistakes, cry, experience pain, then come back here and let me comfort you. I want you to know, both yourself and the world.

Finding god through heresy took the pressure off. I could stop arguing with the text, I could stop arguing with god's earthly self-appointed representatives. It wasn't a relief—when I found gnosticism it wasn't the sensation of being washed over or embraced or of coming home or any of the other metaphors I see when reading about conversion experiences. It was being told that all of the restlessness, all of the seeking, all of the dissatisfaction and work to create meaning, that was the point. That's the job of religion, just keep doing that.

After the man was found, after the ransom was paid and he rejoined our lives, I was still crying in cathedrals but now for different reasons. We had become lovers, but it was disappointing and painful and hard. At least this suffering was mundane, and when I talked about it people immediately understood what I was talking about.

So I found myself on my knees in front of the head of St. Catherine of Siena. I had expected crowds, someone told me there are usually crowds, but the cathedral was empty. It was just me and her incorruptible head and her finger, which was not looking great. I don't know if I was crying for her or for me. I don't know if I envied her sense of purpose or if I felt sorry that her dead body was being put on display by a church that exploited women like her. The best we can ever really do, I guess, is to do the most we can with what we have, and she certainly did that, turning the biological reality of femaleness—usually a form of death—into the life of an intellectual and diplomat and philosopher.

"What are we going to do?" I whispered to her head through the glass. It felt stupid and selfish to take heartbreak to a dead nun, but heartbreak makes selfish idiots of all of us.

The love my favorite nuns had for god was like this exquisite heartbreak, the pain of knowing one is alive, the joy of knowing that being alive means having this capacity for pain. This love, this pain, this yearning, it drove them into the convent, which looked like a refusal of life but was actually its embrace.

But looking to god or a dead nun to tell you what to do is just part of my Protestant training. The knowing of gnosis should feel a lot closer to unknowing or at least uncertainty. It is not a list of tasks to be completed, it is a deep, dark pool. And that is terrifying.

I think of the dark brick church of my childhood, where we dutifully went once a week in itchy clothes and too-tight shoes. Where we were told how terrible the world was, the better to diminish it. Told to create a world out of only what you can control: your family, your domestic scene, your realm. Don't wander, don't look up, don't wonder what else might be possible. The devil might be out there.

Catherine didn't answer me that day, but I hear her, and all of the saints and gods and monsters and devils, whispering and shouting and singing in my ears as I walk through the world. What are we going to do?

We are going to love the man who can't love us back, who scares us with his anger and his pain. And we will be loved by others who we can't love back, and we will scare them with our lack of regard.

We are going to fuck up, endlessly. We are going to get messy, we will scrape our knees, we will fall on our face, knock a tooth loose, get a black eye. Everyone will see this happen; there will be no dignity to hide behind.

We will try and fail to love the world that can't love us back, at least not in a way we can feel and understand.

We will suffer.

We will hurt those who love us, cause enormous amounts of pain, and we will be unable to shield ourselves from the painful love tossed at us in the form of hurtful words and murderous intent.

We will try and fail to see ourselves as we actually are, and not through the distorted mirror of our disappointment. We will see our beauty fade or fail to bloom. We will betray ourselves through envy, poisonous and vain.

We will do as much as we can. We will pursue god in all its forms, and we will despair when it eludes us.

We will turn to the world with loving intention, and then fail to live up to our own expectations. We will overthink things, we will shirk from pure honesty, we will use our hurts and our traumas as excuses for not giving more. We will be selfish and cruel. We will get lost in black clouds. Then we will find our way back to love somehow again.

We will live our lives. And then they will end. It is all any of us can ever do.

[–O]

I have no fear
of this machine

"OH, DID I TELL YOU?"

Nothing good ever follows this question in my family. One time it was "Your father had an abscess on his liver and had to have surgery and almost died, but this was, what, two months ago?" Another time, "Your grandmother kidnapped your grandfather from the hospital because she was lonely, and when he fell out of bed she didn't have enough strength to pick him up, so we found him days later in his own waste." I braced myself.

"We discovered your grandfather is not your grandfather."

My sister had taken the 23 & Me test out of curiosity about our origins, and when she looked on the tab to see what distant family members she might be matched with, fourth cousins eighty times removed or whatever, she found instead a lot of unknown close relatives. I mean, *close*.

"Well, we checked around, we did some digging, and we tried to figure out how our family tree might be crossed with theirs. You know how your father is about genealogy, he has meticulously followed every part of our family, but he had never heard of these people! The one thing we did have in common, though, was our mothers had both visited the same fertility doctor."

You may have read the headlines about a fertility doctor who used his own sperm to impregnate his patients. Well, it wasn't him. Or the other one you heard of. Or that one either. It was an unfamous fertility doctor who did the same thing as a bunch of other fertility doctors. Maybe it hasn't made headlines because now it's so mundane. There were a bunch of men midcentury pumping women full of their genetic material, pretending it was their husband's or an anonymous donor's or a close friend's.

"Did grandma know?"

"Well, she's dead of course, so there's no way of knowing. We never talked about things like this."

It was hard to tell how my mother felt about any of this. She was casual, treating it like a funny anecdote rather than a disruption to our entire sense of who our family was.

It was hard to tell how I felt about any of this. My grandfather was a nonentity during my childhood. He carried some serious damage from World War II, which he discussed only once, when he all of a sudden gave his medals to our cousin one Christmas, along with a letter saying he had been given them for bravery, which seemed stupid to him, because all he had ever been trying to do was not die. Then he clammed up, maybe wandered out of the room. He was always doing that, wandering out, mumbling to himself, shuffling his feet on the carpet and delivering electric shocks when he absentmindedly patted you on your head.

There were hints in the tense conversations I overheard between my aunts and uncles that suggested he had been much different when they were younger. Angry. It would be alluded to but then not spoken of again. The revelation of their biological parentage had been shocking to them, at least. They all seemed to have the same genetic father. My grandmother had gone back to the same doctor, it could be assumed, for each new pregnancy. Some wanted to know these new family members and explore their new connection, others wanted nothing to do with their half-siblings.

My mother showed me pictures of our new relatives. There was a resemblance, I suppose. My sister had been in communication with them, building an emotional connection. I realized in that moment, looking at these pictures, their pasty faces reflecting my pasty face, that I felt the same for them as I did for my extended family. Which is to say, I felt nothing whatsoever.

It shocked me, that this news meant nothing to me. Surely that made me heartless. Surely that made me sociopathic. What are the signs of sociopathy? Tell me, Google. "Glibness and superficial charm"? Well, no, I am quite lacking in charm. "Manipulative and cunning"? Oh, I wish. If that were true my career wouldn't be stalled. "Shallow emotions"? Considering I cried for an hour after the last play I saw in the theater, this is unlikely. Okay, maybe I'm not a sociopath. But surely I should feel something for people I have known all my life. People I grew up around. People I share blood with.

Yet it all felt so arbitrary. Proximity does not necessarily transform into closeness, and genetic bonds do not necessarily transform into connection. And now, looking at our family from this distance, it seemed clear that it was mostly a performance of traditional roles, not a structure of care. My family didn't just have secrets, it had dangers, but admitting those dangers and actively protecting its vulnerable members from them would have meant dropping the performance. And who was the big act for? The community? The neighborhood? The larger family? God?

The whole fantasy of the happy family was only that: a fantasy. Collectively believed in, but insubstantial and nebulous all the same. And one of the fog machines cranking out that fantasy had just sputtered out. Your grandfather is not your grandfather. The grand genetic lineage is broken, the bloodline dried up. It was easier to see how spectral it all is now. It was easier to see what was on the other side of this.

After all, if my family was a series of performances played for the benefit of others, what would happen if I just stopped playing? What would happen if all of us, the drained and the uncared for, the unprotected and the vulnerable, just stopped playing? I don't want anyone to remove their care or tenderness or support or understanding. We need more of that in the world, not less. But to take off masks, to go off-script, to jump off the stage and run into the streets instead.

The advertisements for 23 & Me make it look so harmless. Find out where your DNA comes from! Learn important information about your health, or the health of your future children! Discover distant relatives in other countries who you can drag into your petty dramas!

But in reality, 23 & Me has had to hire crisis counselors to deal with all the trauma it has caused. The brother you grew up with in your cozy little nuclear family listed is suddenly recast as a "half-sibling." People are finding out there is no such thing as racial or national purity. People are finding out their mother was impregnated by sperm that was not their father's. People are finding their relatives implicated in long-ago cold cases, murders and rapes and kidnappings.

Personally, I think they should embrace this. If this is the purpose 23 & Me can serve in our society, let them be proud of it. I imagine a new series of ad campaigns. Find out if your uncle is truly the creep you always thought he was! Discover the real reason you sometimes found your mother crying in the dark! Unlearn racism, by learning you are 10 percent whatever it is you think should be eradicated from the earth!

People are buying these tests for their siblings at Christmas, they're casually taking them themselves, looking for a larger cadre of cousins to invite to family reunions, and what they're actually doing is destabilizing the entire paternalistic system that rules the world. It's almost funny.

What if your father is not your Father? What if he's just someone you love, someone you hate, someone who taught you to fix a leaky faucet and taught you the most important thing to do after you cry is to hide all evidence that you just cried? What if he is just the guy who let you watch R-rated movies when your mother was out of town, who tells bad jokes, and whose eyes glaze over when you try to talk about what you find interesting? What if he's the guy who can't cook, can't dance, and really only calls you when he's lonely? What if he's just the guy you were terrified of, who touched you in wrong ways, both with violence and without? What if he's just the guy who pours a thick crust of sugar onto his grapefruit in the morning and orders his steak well-done?

What if he's just that and not the person whose example you have to follow? Whose version of what makes a person feel happy and successful is something you don't have to mimic or rebel against, but simply to understand as being about him and nothing to do with you? Whose opinions about how you should be living your life can be recognized as old-fashioned and irrelevant? What if he's just a guy who lives in your house?

Like Charlie. I knew how Charlie wanted me to behave, because of the way he'd bang around when I didn't. Stop bringing men home. Stop traveling so much. I felt punished when I transgressed. But it's my home, man. You're dead. You don't get to have any more say. That doesn't mean I think your life had no value, but it was your life and I have no obligation to continue your life into mine. I recognized his oppressive presence as unreasonable. You're dead, Charlie. What makes you think even dead you get a say in how the world works?

I stood in my Kansas City backyard. The forecast was not good. There was an eclipse, we were in the zone of totality, but there were clouds. Maybe it would clear up by the time the eclipse peaked, or maybe I would miss it due to god's whims and have to wait another hundred years for things to align.

I wandered back into the house, I was waiting for someone to come and repair my internet connection. My backyard was somehow a dead zone; my phone could barely get a signal back there. The whole yard felt rotten to me, with its electric fence, its soil that wouldn't grow anything, the mass of mosquitoes that would appear out of nowhere and glom onto my legs and arms the instant I walked outside. I would go outside to check the sky, shake my limbs free of parasites, then go back in to see if the repair man had called yet. It was one of those services where if they call and you don't pick up, they cancel the appointment and you have to wait weeks to reschedule.

Then, suddenly, there was a break in the clouds. I went back outside with my glasses, and I saw the moon overtake the sun. It was almost exact, the world turned uncanny. The unsettling shadows, the eerie stillness as the birds and insects fell silent. Then, it was exact, and I felt my body start to shake. I was weeping. I took off my glasses, and I stared into that dark hole punched in the sky.

Just like that, this inevitable force, this massive presence was gone. Overtaken. Eclipsed. The sun was gone, the moon was an absence, and the world was rendered unfamiliar. It was terrifying. It was awesome.

As the sun began to break through its containment again, the clouds covered it up. The phone rang from the kitchen counter, the repairman was on his way.

But I couldn't stop thinking. The sun can go away. It's possible. It's a thing that happens. I could barely breathe.

Later, months later, I knew I was done. I didn't have to stay in thrall to my dads. I didn't have to stay with Charlie. I got rid of most of my things, gave them away or sold them to neighbors, packed up the rest, and bought a train ticket to Chicago.

My last night there, I felt Charlie restless. I shut myself and my cat away in what had been the library but was now just clean white walls. I couldn't sleep, I felt him skulking around the room. He wanted to make himself felt, he wanted to make his presence known. The cat, normally a free spirit, slept right against my face.

Charlie didn't understand what I finally understood, what took me so long to figure out: I could just leave.

And I did.

Selected Bibliography

FATHER

The Knotted Subject by Elisabeth Bronfen
The Grand Domestic Revolution by Dolores Hayden
Cities of Ladies by Walter Simons
Dark Age Nunneries by Steven Vanderputten
Tragic Ways of Killing a Woman by Nicole Loraux
SQM: The Quantified Home, edited by Space Caviar
Tragedy Is Not Enough by Karl Jaspers
Ties That Bind by Sarah Schulman
How to Mend: Motherhood and Its Ghosts by Iman Mersal
The Delusions of Care by Bonaventure Soh Bejeng Ndikung
Home Re-Assembled: On Art, Destruction, and Belonging

CITIZEN

Age of Anger by Pankaj Mishra
The Need for Roots by Simone Weil
Living My Life by Emma Goldman

On the Irish Freedom Struggle by Bernadette Devlin
A Treatise on Northern Ireland by Brendan O'Leary
The Unnamable Present by Roberto Calasso
To Purge This Land with Blood by Stephen B. Oates
Everybody Talks About the Weather . . . We Don't by Ulrike Meinhof
Inventory by Darran Anderson
A Field Guide for Female Interrogators by Coco Fusco
Civil Wars by Hans Magnus Enzensberger
Visions of Empire by Krishan Kumar

GOD

Eros and Magic in the Renaissance by Ioan Couliano
The Tree of Gnosis by Ioan Couliano
Teresa, My Love by Julia Kristeva
The Enchantments of Mammon by Eugene McCarraher
Luther by Heiko Oberman
Black Athena by Martin Bernal
Seven Types of Atheism by John Gray
Varieties of Religious Experience by William James
Story of a Soul by St. Therese of Lisieux